Recreational Nitrox Diving

BEST PUBLISHING COMPANY

Also by the author...

Dive Like a Pro: 101 Ways to Improve Your Diving Skills and Safety

Exploring Diving: The Diver's Guide to Underwater Training and Adventure

For more information contact:

    Best Publishing Company
    2355 North Steves Boulevard
    P.O. Box 30100
    Flagstaff, AZ 86003-0100
    Email: divebooks@bestpub.com
    Fax: 520.526.0370
    Phone: 800.468.1055 or 520.527.1055

Recreational Nitrox Diving

by

Robert N. Rossier

BEST PUBLISHING COMPANY

Illustrations: Rick Melvin, Divers Alert Network and Curt Bowen, Undersea Breathing
Systems, Inc.

Copyright © 2000 Best Publishing Company

All rights reserved.

No part of this book may be reproduced, stored in a retrieval system or transmitted in any form or by any means — electronic, mechanical, photocopying, microfilming, or otherwise — without written permission from the publisher, except by a reviewer, who may quote brief passages in a review with appropriate credit.

ISBN No.: 0-941332-83-7
LIBRARY OF CONGRESS: 99-068035

Best Publishing Company
2355 North Steves Boulevard
P.O. Box 30100
Flagstaff, AZ 86003-0100 USA

Table of Contents

List of Figures.............................. VII

List of Tables IX

Acknowledgements XI

Introduction XIII

Chapter 1: Why Nitrox?.................... 1

Chapter 2: The Physiology of
            Nitrox Diving................... 9

Chapter 3: Nitrox Dive Planning 29

Chapter 4: Equipment Requirements........ 47

Chapter 5: Procedures and Safeguards 51

Chapter 6: How Nitrox is Made 59

Chapter 7: Safe Diving Considerations 69

Glossary 73

References and Resources.................. 79

List of Figures

Partial Pressure and Gas Diffusion 12

Some Predisposing Factors in Oxygen Toxicity 22

Labeling of Nitrox Cylinders 52

Oxygen Service Label 53

Contents Tag or Sticker .53

Verifying the Oxygen Content of a Nitrox Cylinder After Receiving a Fill 55

A Hyperfiltration System is Used to Produce Oxygen Compatible Air .60

A Technician Uses Partial Pressure Blending to Fill a Nitrox Cylinder 62

Typical Pressure Swing Absorption (PSA) System 65

Typical DeNitrogenated Air (DNAx) System . . .66

List of Tables

Total Pressure and Oxygen Partial
Pressure (PO_2) for Air at Depth 10

Physiological Effects of Hypoxic
Breathing Mixtures 14

Oxygen Exposure Limits (NOAA, 2000) 23

Repex Oxygen Exposure (NOAA, 2000) 26

Maximum Oxygen Exposure Limits for
Pulmonary Oxygen Toxicity (NOAA, 2000) 27

Best Mix Recreational Nitrox (EAN) 32

MOD (fsw) for Recreational Nitrox 37

EAD for Recreational Nitrox Mixtures 39

This book is dedicated to the memory of my father, Roland T. Rossier, who not only provided encouragement and support in all my endeavors, but served as an outstanding role model.

ACKNOWLEDGEMENTS

Preparing a book for publication is always a much more demanding task than one first imagines, but when the subject matter is as crucial as diving technology, the end never seems to come. As with all such efforts, a great number of individuals contributed in one way or another to the development of this book. A significant portion of the material included in this book was first developed for publication in Alert Diver, the magazine of Divers Alert Network (DAN). Special recognition and thanks are due to Dr. Ed Thalmann, DAN's Associate Medical Director, whose ongoing efforts in the field of diving and hyperbaric medicine contributed directly to portions of this book. Dr. Thalmann also provided a critical review of the manuscript. Additional thanks are due to Renee Westerfield and Barry Shuster of DAN for their guidance and technical assistance, and to Rick Melvin for the use of his illustrations.

Numerous individuals and organizations provided technical support including Alex Brylske of Dive Training magazine, Michael Casey II of Lawrence Factor, Gary Clark of SSI, Bill Delp of Underwater Breathing Systems, Duard Hardy of Infusion Systems, and Ed Rosacker of Diver's Cove Dive Center. My sincere thanks to these fine individuals and all others who provided information and assistance either directly or indirectly.

I wish to thank Jim and Susan Joiner and the staff of Best Publishing. Jim and Susan provided both encouragement and technical support, and their professional staff brought the manuscript to life in print.

I could never have completed this project without the love and support of my wife, Lori, who not only helped me find the time to write and research, but who reviewed and edited the manuscript. Finally, I want to thanks the two greatest kids in the world, Rachel and Ethan, for providing the much needed diversions throughout the process of preparing the manuscript.

DISCLAIMER

Scuba diving involves inherent risks that must be accepted by any individual engaging in the sport. Neither the author nor publisher accepts responsibility for accidents or injuries resulting from the use of materials contained herein. The information in this book pertains to open-circuit scuba diving with nitrox, and should be considered a supplement to an approved nitrox diving training program provided by a nationally recognized scuba certification agency. This book cannot take the place of training provided by a professional instructor. All certificated divers should receive professional instruction and certification in nitrox diving before attempting to dive with any breathing mixtures including nitrox.

In addition to the information contained herein, all divers should follow the safe diving rules, practices and procedures taught at every level of scuba certification. Professional training, certification, routine review of diving skills and knowledge, and adherence to conservative diving practices and procedures are necessary ingredients for safe recreational diving, regardless of the breathing mixture used.

INTRODUCTION

They say you can't teach an old dog new tricks, but the truth is there's a certain comfort level that comes from familiarity, a confidence that lies in going to the same place, using the same tools, or following the same procedure time after time. That's why it's scary when we start a new job, why we accidentally turn on the wipers instead of the headlights in a rental car, or why we fumble when trying to eat with our fork in the wrong hand.

So it is with diving. I like my BC, not because it's the best one made, but because I've used it so often. I don't fumble trying to find the inflator, cinch a strap, or open a pocket. My console always hangs in the same spot, so I know where to look. Because I was so familiar with diving a certain way, with certain equipment, and following known procedures, I was tentative about switching to nitrox. After all, I'm comfortable with air. I've been breathing it all my life.

The term "nitrox" smacks of technical diving, and many divers have preconceived notions about the subject. Nitrox diving is often viewed as a new frontier that lies beyond recreational diving. Concerns arise about the need for special equipment, techniques and procedures. Many view nitrox diving as highly complex, providing numerous opportunities for divers to put themselves at increased risk.

In spite of these preconceived notions, nitrox has gained wide acceptance in the recreational diving community over the past few decades. While it is widely used by the military as well as technical, commercial and scientific divers, the techniques, procedures and tables have been refined to the point that with a modicum of training, nitrox diving can be safe and enjoyable for the recreational open-circuit scuba diver. Still, there's much to be considered, a lot to be weighed, before changing to nitrox. Before you decide to dive with nitrox, it's critical to understand the potential risks and benefits. Should you choose to dive nitrox, professional training is an absolute necessity.

The purpose of this book is to provide the recreational diver with a basic understanding of the concepts and principles involved in nitrox diving with open-circuit scuba. Every effort has been made to provide this information in a logical, simple, and easily understood format.

CHAPTER 1

Why Nitrox?

The popularity of nitrox diving is growing by leaps and bounds, and there are many reasons why recreational divers are considering nitrox for open-circuit scuba. It can offer several important advantages, and if used properly, may even reduce certain risks in recreational diving. On the other hand, the use of nitrox does entail certain complexities and considerations beyond those associated with breathing compressed air. Before we explore the use of nitrox in detail, it's important to understand exactly what nitrox is, its history and track record in diving, and some overriding operational considerations in its use.

1.1 NITROX DEFINED

The term "Nitrox" is often used to refer to any breathing mixture consisting primarily of nitrogen and oxygen. More specifically, nitrox is any prepared oxygen-nitrogen breathing gas in which one or more components have been added or modified, i.e. compressed ambient air is not technically nitrox. Nitrox used in recreational diving goes by several pseudonyms, including SafeAir (a copyrighted term used by American Nitrox Divers, Inc., or ANDI), oxygen-enriched air, and EAN for Enriched Air Nitrox. Nitrox can have 21 percent oxygen, in which case it is used just like air. Nitrox can also have more than the roughly 21 percent oxygen found in normal air, or it can have less. Nitrox is often labeled as EANx, with the "x" standing for the percentage of oxygen in the mixture.

The oxygen fraction of recreational nitrox mixtures generally ranges from 22 percent to 40 percent. Specific mixtures are referred to as NN32 (EAN32, or 32 percent oxygen, and formerly referred to as NOAA Nitrox I) and NN36 (EAN36, or 36 percent oxygen, and formerly referred to as NOAA Nitrox II).

1.2 THE HISTORY OF NITROX IN RECREATIONAL DIVING

While the use of nitrox in recreational diving is relatively new dating to the mid 1980s, nitrox has been used in other forms of diving literally for decades. One of the most prominent figures in recreational nitrox is diving pioneer Dick Rutkowski. As director of dive training for the National Oceanic and Atmospheric Administration (NOAA, formerly the Environmental Science Services Administration or ESSA) from 1965 to 1985, Rutkowski helped pioneer the use of nitrox for scientific, research and commercial diving applications. Rutkowski retired from NOAA in 1985, began teaching nitrox diving in the recreational diving world, and founded the International Association of Nitrox and Technical Divers (IANTD) in 1986. In 1988, he co-founded another nitrox certification agency: American Nitrox Divers, International (ANDI).

Nearly all scuba certification agencies including NASDS, NAUI, PADI, SSI and YMCA have now embraced nitrox and offer nitrox certification courses for certified divers. According to one informal poll, the number of certified nitrox divers in the U.S. is well over the 100,000 mark, with nearly 10,000 instructors providing basic nitrox training. Nitrox and nitrox training is available virtually world wide in a growing percentage of dive centers, resorts and dive vessels. Nitrox fills are widely available and usually cost just a few dollars more than standard air fills.

1.3 OPERATIONAL CONSIDERATIONS IN NITROX DIVING

An important exercise for any diver considering the switch to nitrox is to carefully sift through the advantages and potential risks. In many instances, nitrox is a two-edged sword with the potential for both increased safety and increased risk. Nitrox should perhaps be considered as a diving tool, which carries with it a different set of advantages and disadvantages than compressed air. In this section we'll review a number of the common myths and misconceptions, and separate the myth from the math.

1.3.1 NITROX LIMITS

A common misconception about nitrox is that it is used for deep diving. In reality, the increased oxygen content means that certain nitrox mixtures are actually limited to shallower depths than air due to the increased risk of oxygen toxicity. (see Chapter 2) However, nitrox mixtures, although not ALL nitrox mixtures, are well suited to the recreational diving depths.

In some cases, nitrox can increase your bottom time. If your bottom time is limited by no-decompression limits, you may be able to extend your bottom time by using nitrox rather than air. Other factors may also play into the bottom time equation, including thermal exposure, fatigue, etc.

Another potential advantage to nitrox is shorter surface intervals compared to the same dive profiles when using air. Since we absorb less nitrogen when breathing nitrox, it takes less time to offgas residual nitrogen in preparation for a second dive. Thus, nitrox effectively reduces the required surface interval between dives by allowing divers to take advantage of their reduced equivalent air depth (EAD). Many divers follow the standard (air) no-decompression tables and thus begin their repetitive dives in a lower repetitive dive group. This may provide an increased margin of safety against decompression illness (DCI).

1.3.2 MEDICAL CONSIDERATIONS

Another myth regarding nitrox is that divers cannot get bent when using nitrox. Although using nitrox while following the no-decompression limits (NDL's) for an air dive can provide an increased safety margin against DCI, nitrox divers can get bent just as readily as air divers can. Nitrox divers must follow appropriate dive tables (or a nitrox computer) to avoid exceeding the established no-decompression limits (NDL's). Furthermore, nitrox divers are urged to follow the same conservative practices heralded by their air-breathing counterparts. (See Chapter 7)

Some divers have the misconception that nitrox divers can't be treated in a recompression chamber. This is myth again. Nitrox divers can be treated just as readily as divers breathing compressed air can. Hyperbaric treatment of recreational divers breathing air or nitrox is based on symptoms, not the specific breathing gas used on a dive.

Some divers claim to feel less "narked" while using nitrox, however there is little scientific evidence to prove this claim. Some experts suggest quite the opposite, that the increased partial pressure of oxygen has a euphoric effect which seems to negate the effect of reduced nitrogen partial pressure.

1.3.3 PROCEDURES AND EQUIPMENT FOR NITROX DIVING

Recreational nitrox diving is actually relatively simple, but it does require a few additional considerations beyond those commonly associated with breathing compressed air. Just as recreational air divers must consider the potential for decompression sickness, nitrox divers must, in addition, consider the potential for oxygen toxicity. While nitrox can be used safely, and may reduce the risk of DCI if air diving tables are used, the opposite side of the safety coin is the potential for oxygen toxicity. The risk of oxygen toxicity is essentially zero while breathing compressed air within the 130 foot recreational diving limit. However, oxygen toxicity is a potential risk when using some nitrox mixtures even at recreational diving depths. Some nitrox mixtures can only be used safely to a depth of 80 feet under some conditions. Some simple arithmetic and published tables are used to ensure the oxygen limits for single and repetitive nitrox dives are not exceeded. Through this planning, the risk of oxygen toxicity can be all but eliminated.

With only a couple minor exceptions, recreational nitrox diving can be done using the same equipment used for diving with compressed air. A cylinder used for nitrox must be oxygen cleaned appropriately for its intended use and must bear the proper identification labeling it as safe for nitrox. (See Chapters 4 and 5) If you plan to extend your bottom time through the use of nitrox, you may want a larger cylinder. Swapping your aluminum 80 for steel 100 might pose little problem on a boat dive, but consider the additional weight carefully when contemplating a tough beach or surf entry.

Verifying the contents of a nitrox cylinder prior to a dive is an important safety procedure since different mixtures or "blends" carry different operating limitations. The prudent diver will have his or her own oxygen analyzer to verify the nitrox blend before diving.

Some divers prefer a dive computer to the use of tables. Numerous dive computers are available that accommodate nitrox diving. Some can be used for air or nitrox. (See Chapter 4) The rest of your equipment, including regulator, BC, and pressure gages are all acceptable for use with recreational nitrox mixtures.

Nitrox is becoming more and more available every year. Many dive resorts and liveaboard dive vessels now offer nitrox, and the number is growing steadily. In addition, equipment is now available to make it economical for dive center operators and specially trained divers to prepare nitrox in relatively small quantities. For more information see Chapter 6.

1.4 BALANCING THE SAFETY EQUATION

There is currently much debate regarding the safety of nitrox diving relative to using compressed air. Our current understanding of decompression illness (DCI) suggests that exposure to nitrogen is the primary factor in determining the risk of developing symptoms. If a breathing gas with a lower fraction of nitrogen is used on the same dive profile as an air dive, it stands to reason that the risk of DCI is reduced. That is, if we follow the air tables using nitrox, the potential for DCI is less. If we calculate the equivalent air depth (EAD) for our nitrox blend and dive to the no-decompression limit (NDL) for that depth, our risk is probably similar to that of a dive to the same depth and NDL using air.

Since we don't know how many recreational divers are using nitrox versus air, and we don't have a complete database of diving injuries, it is difficult to assess the relative safety of nitrox versus air diving. However, according to a report published by the Divers Alert Network (DAN), injuries reported among nitrox and other mixed gas users are similar in type and distribution to those reported using air. Of the reported injuries, 65.2 percent were neurologic injuries (DCS Type II) for nitrox/mixed gas, compared to 62.7 percent for air diving. There were no reported cases of arterial gas embolism (AGE) for the nitrox/mixed gas community; a phenomenon potentially attributed to the higher experience level of most nitrox/mixed gas divers. Thus it appears at first blush that nitrox is at least as safe as air when properly used.

The use of nitrox computers can significantly reduce the potential human errors associated with mathematical computation and table reading. The only caveat is that divers using nitrox computers must program in additional parameters (e.g. the oxygen fraction of their nitrox blend) not required for air computers.

As long as we follow the recommended limits and established procedures, we can virtually eliminate the hazard of oxygen toxicity when diving with nitrox. Nitrox divers must adhere to the maximum operating depth (MOD) limitations for their nitrox mixtures, and verify the mixture in their breathing gas cylinders through the use of a gas analyzer. Failure to follow these simple precautions is as risky as diving without a depth gauge.

Diving with nitrox can improve our safety and enjoyment of recreational diving as long as we follow established protocol and abide by conservative diving practices. (See Chapter 7) Just remember that diving is not a risk free sport and lapses of judgment or disregard of procedures and protocols can result in serious consequences. Grab the wrong cylinder when you're suiting up, and you could come back bent like a pretzel. Be sloppy with the math, read the tables incorrectly, improperly analyze the mixture in your cylinder, or improperly program your nitrox computer and the risk of injury skyrockets. Only by following established procedures, precautions, and protocols for recreational nitrox diving can we avoid such mistakes.

Nitrox diving with open-circuit scuba is not overly complex, and many divers enjoy the potential advantages of extended bottom times, reduced surface intervals, or the added protection against DCI offered by nitrox. In the following chapters, we'll explore each of the considerations in more detail, and clearly map out the procedures, safeguards and techniques that can make recreational open-circuit nitrox diving safe and enjoyable.

Notes

CHAPTER 2

The Physiology of Nitrox Diving

To safely dive with nitrox, it's important to understand the physiological implications of breathing a gas mixture with non-standard proportions of nitrogen and oxygen. In this chapter, we'll review the basic physics and physiology that form the foundation of recreational nitrox diving.

2.1 PARTIAL PRESSURES

The key to understanding the physiology of nitrox diving is the concept of partial pressures. Our physiological response to a gas is determined not so much by the percentage of a gas in the breathing mixture as its partial pressure. When we talk about the effects of various breathing gases on our physiology, we'll speak in terms of partial pressures.

Remember that the partial pressure is the fraction of the total pressure represented by the fraction of the gas in the mixture (Dalton's Law). If a gas mixture is 32 percent oxygen, then the oxygen exerts 32 percent of the total pressure. If the total pressure is 100 psi, the partial pressure of the oxygen is 32 psi.

TABLE 2-1
TOTAL PRESSURE AND OXYGEN PARTIAL PRESSURE (PO_2) FOR AIR AT DEPTH

Depth (FSW)	Total Pressure (ATA)	PO_2 (ATA)
0 (sea level)	1.0	0.21
33	2.0	0.42
66	3.0	0.63
99	4.0	0.84
132	5.0	1.05

Numerous units of measurement are commonly used to express pressure. These include psi, Bar, Torr, feet of seawater (FSW), millimeters of mercury (mmHg) and Atmospheres Absolute (ATA). Cylinder pressure is measured in either psig or Bar. For the purposes of discussing physiological effects of breathing gasses on divers, the most appropriate units of pressure measurement are mmHg and ATA.

The standard sea level pressure is 1 ATA. Considering that ambient air is roughly 21 percent oxygen, the air we breathe at the surface has an oxygen partial pressure (PO_2) of .21 ATA. At a depth of 33 feet in seawater (fsw), the ambient pressure is double, or 2 ATA, and the corresponding oxygen partial pressure is 0.42 ATA. At 66 FSW, the ambient pressure is triple that of the surface (3 ATA), and the oxygen partial pressure is 0.63 ATA.

2.2 GAS DIFFUSION

The importance of partial pressure in diving is that it determines the rate of gas diffusion into and out of the body's tissues (see Figure 2-1). The rate at which gasses diffuse into and out of human tissues is determined by a number of factors, including the partial pressure of the breathing gas and the partial pressure or "tension" of the gas dissolved in the tissue. The partial pressure of the breathing gas depends on the depth (total pressure) and the fraction of the gas in the breathing mixture. The deeper we go, the greater the total pressure, and hence the greater the partial pressures of the gas we breathe. If we increase the percentage of oxygen in our breathing mixture, we likewise reduce the percentage of nitrogen in the breathing gas, and thus we reduce the partial pressure of nitrogen.

The amount of gas that can dissolve in our tissues, or the equilibrium tension of a dissolved gas in our tissues, also depends on a number of factors. Most important is the partial pressure of the breathing gas. As we increase the partial pressure of a gas such as nitrogen by diving to a greater depth, the total amount of nitrogen that can dissolve into our tissues increases. At every depth, there is a "saturation" point, or an equilibrium gas tension that will be reached after a sufficient period of time at that depth.

Temperature can also affect the diffusion of gas into and out of tissues. More gas can dissolve into the tissues when the temperature is lower, however human physiology is more complex than the simple gas/water interface used to illustrate textbook examples. In a diver's body, temperature affects gas diffusion indirectly in a myriad of ways such as changes in the blood flow and circulation in various tissues in response to cold. Blood chemistry, hydration, exercise, and a host of other physiological factors also affect the rate of gas diffusion into and out of tissues.

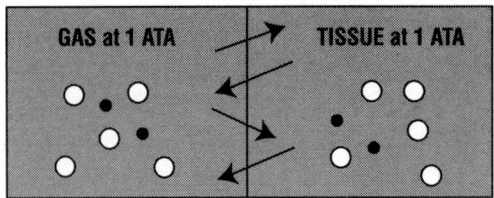

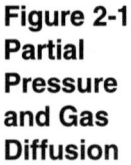

Figure 2-1 Partial Pressure and Gas Diffusion

Figure 2-1a. The tissue is in equilibrium with the gas when the rate of diffusion into the tissue equals the rate of diffusion out of the tissue.

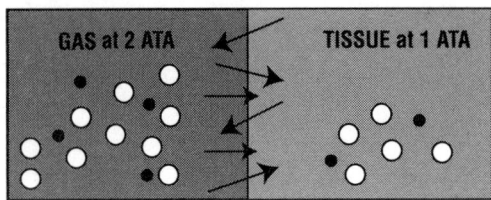

Figure 2-1b. By increasing the partial pressure of the gas, we increase the rate of diffusion into the tissue until the gas tension of the tissue reaches a new equilibrium. In other words, more gas can diffuse into the tissue when the partial pressure of the gas is increased.

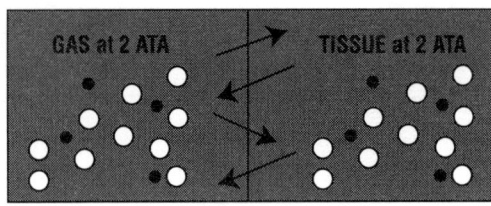

Figure 2-1c. All things being equal, a tissue can hold more gas when it is cold. In the human body, many other factors influence gas diffusion into and out of the tissues. For example, decreasing temperature also alters blood circulation, which influences gas diffusion to a much greater degree than temperature alone.

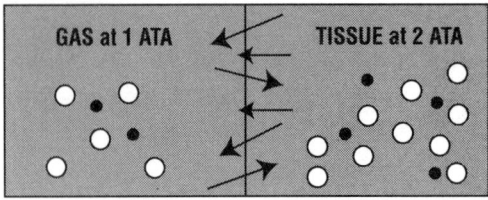

Figure 2-1d. By reducing the partial pressure of nitrogen in the breathing gas, we can decrease the diffusion rate of nitrogen into the tissue, and lower the equilibrium nitrogen tension for any depth.

2.3 THE ROLE OF NITROGEN

Nitrogen is generally considered an inert gas, and while this is technically true, divers are probably more aware of the physiological effects of nitrogen than of any other gas. Although the body does not metabolize nitrogen, its effects on the diver are well known.

Nitrogen enters and leaves the body via the pulmonary system (the lungs). At normal pressures, the rate of nitrogen entering and leaving the body are the same. However, as pressures increase, the nitrogen tension of our blood and tissues increases until a new saturation tension is achieved. If the pressure is then reduced, the process reverses with nitrogen exiting the body via the lungs until a new equilibrium is established. If the saturation tension of nitrogen is achieved as the pressure is reduced, bubble formation may occur, resulting in the bends.

At depths greater than about 100 fsw, nitrogen has a narcotic effect referred to a nitrogen narcosis, which seriously degrades a diver's judgment, reaction time, and motor coordination. At greater depths, these effects become more pronounced and can result in serious consequences. Below 250 to 300 fsw, divers may experience convulsions and lose consciousness as a result of nitrogen narcosis.

2.4 THE ROLE OF OXYGEN

Oxygen is a vital element. It provides the chemical energy that sustains the processes of human life. While our ability to survive without food is measured in weeks, and our ability to survive without water is measures in days, our ability to survive without oxygen is measured in mere minutes. Without adequate oxygenation of our tissues, irreparable brain damage occurs in a very short period.

The human body is designed to operate efficiently when the partial pressure of oxygen in the air we breathe is approximately 0.21 ATA (21 percent oxygen at standard atmospheric pressure).

TABLE 2-2
PHYSIOLOGICAL EFFECTS OF HYPOXIC BREATHING MIXTURES

Partial Pressure (ATA)	Physiological Effect
0.16 - 0.18	Increased breathing rate, lack of coordination
0.14 - 0.16	Easily tired, emotionally upset, possible loss of feeling of pain on injury, abnormal fatigue from exertion
0.10 - 0.14	Lethargic, apathetic, confused thinking, physical collapse, unconsciousness, nausea, vomiting
Below 0.10	Convulsive movements, gasping, cessation of breathing

This is referred to as a "normoxic" mixture. When the oxygen partial pressure is less than 0.21 ATA, the mixture is referred to as "hypoxic." As the partial pressure of oxygen in the breathing mixture decreases, our ability to function deteriorates (see Table 2-2). Breathing a mixture roughly 0.12 ATA oxygen, an unacclimated human will lose consciousness in about 10 minutes.

A hyperoxic mixture is one with an oxygen partial pressure greater than 0.21 ATA. Hyperoxic breathing mixtures (and in some cases pure O_2) can provide medical benefit, and are used to treat decompression sickness, carbon monoxide poisoning, gangrene, and other maladies. In addition, some aspects of human performance may actually improve with hyperoxic breathing gasses. However, there is a practical limit beyond which the increased partial pressure of oxygen results in toxic effects. This phenomenon is referred to as oxygen toxicity, or "oxtox."

Of particular relevance in understanding the effects of nitrox is the process of oxygen transport in the human body. Oxygen enters the body via the dead-ended portions of the lungs called alveoli. Here, oxygen molecules diffuse across the alveolar membrane into a vast network of capillaries. The area of the alveolar surface across which this diffusion takes place is roughly 70 square meters, however the thickness of the membrane is microscopic. Once the oxygen molecules diffuse across the membrane, they dissolve into the blood and displace carbon dioxide molecules to chemically combine with the blood hemoglobin. Nearly all the oxygen transported by the blood is chemically combined with hemoglobin. Only about 1/65 of the oxygen is transported in dissolved form in the blood plasma. The oxygen tension of the blood leaving the lungs is in the order of 100 mmHg (0.13 ATA). The CO_2 tension of blood leaving the lungs is in the order of 40 mmHg (0.05 ATA).

The oxygenated blood flows via the pulmonary veins to the left atrium of the heart, then into the left ventricle, and then via the aorta to the vast system of arteries which supply oxygen-rich blood to the various tissues and organs. As the blood flows through tiny capillaries supplying the tissues and organs, oxygen diffuses across capillary membranes into individual cells. CO_2 diffuses out of the cells and into the capillaries where it replaces the oxygen and combines with the hemoglobin to form carboxyhemoglobin. The blood returning from the body's tissues and organs has an oxygen tension of roughly 40 mmHg (0.05 ATA), and a CO_2 tension of about 46 mmHg (0.06 ATA).

2.5 SHIFTING THE BALANCE: HOW NITROX WORKS

The use of nitrox as a breathing gas provides two advantages in terms of reducing the amount of nitrogen in our body. First, since the partial pressure of a gas is a primary factor in determining the rate of gas diffusion into and out of the body tissues, we can influence the gas diffusion rate by adjusting the partial pressure of gas in the breathing mixture. By reducing the partial pressure of nitrogen in our breathing gas and replacing it with more oxygen, we slow the rate of nitrogen diffusion into the tissues. Therefore, we can remain at depth for a longer period of time before reaching the saturation point that defines our no-decompression limit (NDL). Furthermore, the gas tension at equilibrium is lower than it would be for the same depth when breathing compressed air. So, in terms of nitrogen absorption, breathing nitrox has a similar effect as diving to a shallower depth with compressed air.

In addition, the increased fraction of oxygen in the breathing gas helps eliminate nitrogen from the body. Since CO_2 is much more soluble in blood than oxygen, an equivalent number of CO_2 molecules can be transported at a lower partial pressure or tension. As we increase the arterial oxygen partial pressure, the CO_2 tension of the venous blood increases by a lower percentage. So, increasing arterial oxygen tension results in a decreased venous gas tension, thus allowing more nitrogen to dissolve into the venous blood and be transported to the lungs. For this reason, the use of nitrox speeds the elimination of nitrogen from the body during ascents, and during safety/decompression stops.

2.6 THE DARK SIDE OF NITROX: OXYGEN TOXICITY

In basic open water training, divers are briefly introduced to the concept of oxygen toxicity. We learn that the symptoms of oxygen toxicity occur in the range of about 2 atmospheres absolute (ATA) oxygen partial pressure. To suffer the effects, a diver breathing air would have to reach depths of more than 200 feet/61 meters and well beyond the limits of recreational diving. Although the potential for experiencing oxygen toxicity is essentially nil for a recreational diver breathing compressed air, all this changes when we increase the oxygen percentage of our breathing mixture.

When breathing enriched air nitrox, it is possible to experience oxygen toxicity at recreational diving depths. For example, if we're breathing EAN 40 (40 percent oxygen) at a depth of 130 feet, we experience an oxygen partial pressure of roughly 2.0 ATA. More importantly, research indicates that under many conditions oxygen toxicity can occur at partial pressures as low as 1.4 ATA.

The most hotly debated controversies in nitrox diving revolve around the issues of oxygen toxicity, and selecting safe oxygen exposure limits. At the roots of the controversies lie a plethora of research data which is both complex and convoluted, and the issues are more pressing when one considers the insidious nature with which oxtox strikes.

2.6.1 THE EFFECTS OF OXYGEN TOXICITY

Oxygen toxicity is not a single effect. The term actually refers to a broad spectrum of symptoms and effects. The first category is what we call central nervous system (CNS) oxygen toxicity. Referred to as the Paul Bert Effect in honor of one of the early (late 1800s) oxtox researchers, CNS oxygen toxicity is characterized by any number of debilitating symptoms. These include tunnel vision, ringing of the ears, muscular twitching (particularly of the lips), dizziness, and nausea. At the potentially fatal end of the CNS oxygen toxicity spectrum is a loss of consciousness and convulsions similar to a grand mal seizure. While the convulsions themselves are not necessarily life threatening, when the symptoms occur in the underwater environment, serious trauma or drowning can result. A convulsing diver is likely to thrash around, spit out his regulator and drown in the course of the convulsion. CNS oxygen toxicity occurs with relatively short exposures to high oxygen partial pressures.

A second category of oxtox symptoms is referred to as pulmonary oxygen toxicity, whole body oxygen toxicity, chronic toxicity, or the Lorrain Smith Effect, in honor of another late 1800s oxygen toxicity researcher. Smith noted the toxic effects of moderately high oxygen partial pressures on laboratory mice. Pulmonary oxygen toxicity manifests as damage to the lung tissue and causes symptoms similar in nature to the flu or pneumonia. These symptoms can include coughing, difficulty breathing, lack of coordination, and a sore throat and chest. Pulmonary oxygen toxicity results from a prolonged exposure to moderate oxygen partial pressures, and is generally considered a low risk for recreational nitrox divers. However, instructors and guides who dive nitrox day in and day out may in fact be at slight risk for pulmonary oxygen toxicity, especially if they push the limits. Similarly, recreational nitrox divers making multiple-day repetitive dives for an extended period may also be at risk.

2.6.2 THE MECHANISMS OF OXYGEN TOXICITY

The mechanisms of oxygen toxicity are only beginning to be understood, but according to researchers at the Divers Alert Network (DAN), it appears that at least part of the mechanism occurs at the cellular level. The "powerplant" of all living cells is a structure referred to as the mitochondria. This cellular "organ" biochemically rips apart oxygen molecules and recombines the oxygen atoms with hydrogen atoms to form water and release the energy needed to support all life functions. In this process of rearranging molecules, an extra electron is hooked onto the oxygen forming what is referred to as a superoxide anion.

As explained by DAN's Associate Medical Director, Dr. Ed Thalmann, in an article appearing in Alert Diver, superoxide anions are nothing to fool around with. If left unattended, these highly energized bad actors will react with virtually any other molecule, and the results aren't very pretty. To prevent stray reactions, a host of other chemicals are at the ready to jump in and react with any loose superoxide anions that may appear on the scene. But as oxygen levels in the cell increase, the rate of reaction increases until the demand for protective chemical reactions has exceeded the supply. That's when trouble begins. It is thought that overwhelming the ability of this reaction to neutralize the toxic molecules is responsible, at least in part, for the altercations in central nervous system function characteristic of oxygen toxicity.

The superoxide anion problem is only one biochemical process affected by an increase in oxygen levels in the body. The delicate balance of many biochemical processes may be altered as the normal oxygen levels are exceeded. As protective mechanisms become overwhelmed with increasing exposure to elevated oxygen levels, the results often manifest in some form of "toxic" effects.

2.7 CNS OXTOX AND OXYGEN EXPOSURE LIMITS

There is no definitive exposure limit at which oxygen toxicity occurs, no magic formula to determine exactly when it will strike. In fact, studies conducted over the past several decades show an uncanny variation in both the exposure at which the symptoms occur, and the sequence in which particular symptoms might appear.

2.7.1 OXTOX RESEARCH

It would be nice to have a simple formula relating PO_2, duration of exposure, and the onset of symptoms. For any PO_2, we would expect to find a measurable "safe" time before the onset of symptoms occurs. Using this "black and white" formula, we could calculate with certainty the maximum depth and time limits for a nitrox mixture. In reality, extensive scientific research performed over the past fifty years shows a highly variable pattern of dose or exposure relationship which becomes progressively more difficult to characterize as we introduce the many variables common to diving. Rather than a simple "black and white" formula, we find a large gray area when it comes to the onset and progression of oxygen toxicity symptoms.

What the research data reveals is an alarmingly wide variation in time before the onset of symptoms at any given PO_2. The British Royal Navy under the direction of Dr. Kenneth Donald performed some of the earliest research on oxtox during WWII.

In one classic experiment, a diver repeated the same exposure (70 feet/21 meters, 65 degrees F/18C, at rest breathing 100 percent oxygen) twice a week for three months, and the onset of symptoms varied from 7 minutes to 148 minutes!

We would also like to think that the onset of oxygen toxicity symptoms follows a recognizable pattern. Again, research reveals a wide variability in the onset of oxtox symptoms. In some cases, serious symptoms like convulsions are preceded by less debilitating telltale symptoms such as tingling and muscle twitching. In other cases, the diver becomes convulsive with no warning signs or symptoms. If a diver breathing from a regulator convulses underwater, it is very likely that he will spit out the regulator and drown.

Part of the problem in defining safe PO_2 limits is the variability in the oxtox symptoms. Symptoms such as convulsions are an obvious and clear sign of oxtox. Other symptoms considered "definite" signs of oxtox include muscle twitching, tinnitus (ringing in the ears), blurred or tunnel vision, disorientation, the inability to convey coherent thoughts through speaking (aphasia), rapid side-to-side motions of the eye (nystagmus), and incoordination. Still other symptoms are considered probable; that is, they may be the result of oxtox or some other diving-related malady. Probable symptoms include light-headedness, apprehension, passing nausea, lethargy, and general malaise or dysphporia (not feeling "right"). In other words, it can be difficult to know for certain when a diver is experiencing oxtox symptoms, and this problem has confounded researchers.

Research completed by Dr. Andrea Harabin of the Naval Medical Research Institute (NMRI) in Bethesda, Maryland in the early 90s has helped shed light on the oxtox problem, and provided information helpful in determining safe oxygen exposure limits. Using a mathematical model to analyze research data accumulated by the Navy Experimental Diving Unit (NEDU), she was able to compute the probability of occurrence of CNS oxygen toxicity symptoms. When she included all symptoms (definite and probable) the model determined a CNS oxtox threshold of 1.3 ATA; that is, the probability of CNS oxtox symptoms occurring at or below this level should be essentially zero. When she analyzed the data using only definite symptoms, the model found a CNS oxtox threshold of 1.7 ATA; meaning "definite" symptoms are unlikely to occur at or below 1.7 ATA.

To add further fuel to the oxtox fire, an exercising diver breathing oxygen at 1.6 ATA for 40 minutes suffered an oxtox convulsion at Duke University's F.G. Hall Hypo/Hyperbaric Center. In light of this report, it appears that the 1.6 ATA limit is not overly conservative, and some experts suggest the 1.6 ATA limit should only be used for a diver at rest.

While ongoing studies and research confirm the high degree of variability in oxtox symptoms, the results are useful in establishing a gray area or cautionary zone between "safe" limits and definite danger for recreational nitrox diving. At or below 1.3 ATA, the onset of symptoms appears to be unlikely. At 1.6 ATA and above, divers can expect to suffer potentially life-threatening oxtox symptoms. Between 1.3 and 1.6 ATA is a crapshoot.

2.7.2 PREDISPOSING FACTORS

As with decompression illness, numerous factors are involved, a number of which can predispose us to the problem of oxtox. Thermal stress, individual physiology, drugs, medication, depth, and physical exertion are a few of the more dominant factors that can predispose divers to oxygen toxicity. For this reason, divers must carefully weigh the potential risks when selecting maximum oxygen exposure limits for their dives.

An important point to recognize is that it is virtually impossible to establish "personal" oxygen exposure limits. Our personal oxygen tolerance limits can vary dramatically from one day to the next, or one dive to the next, and there is no way to know what our limit might be on a particular day or dive. Instead, we must look at the available data, and set limits which (we hope) will be safe regardless of our personal variations in oxygen tolerance.

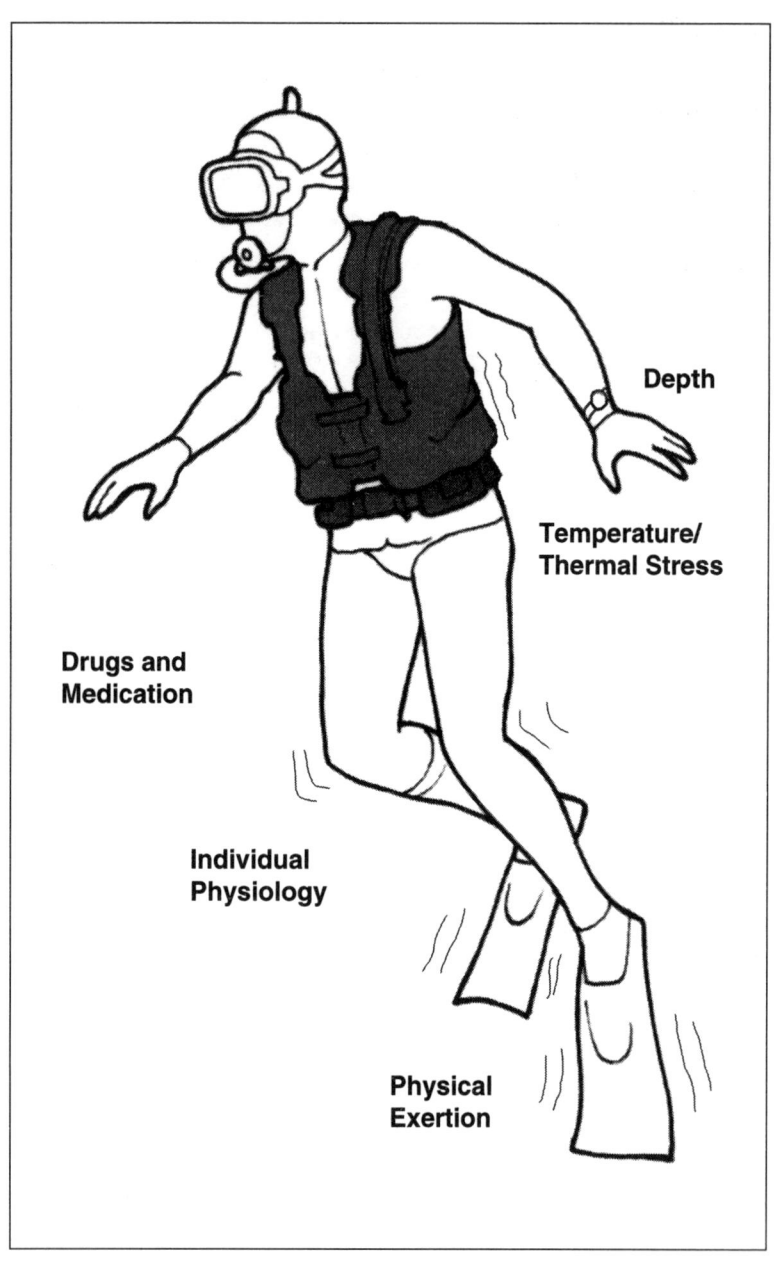

**Figure 2-2
Some Predisposing Factors in Oxygen Toxicity**

2.7.3 SETTING LIMITS FOR OXYGEN EXPOSURE

CNS oxygen exposure limits are defined both in terms of a maximum PO_2, or maximum partial pressure of oxygen, and the duration of the dive. These two factors (dose and time) establish our "exposure" for a particular dive. As the dives become longer in duration, the PO_2 must be more conservative. In addition to limiting the maximum PO_2, it is critical that the exposure time be limited.

TABLE 2-3
OXYGEN EXPOSURE LIMITS (NOAA, 2000)

PO_2 (ATA)	Maximum Single Dive Exposure Limit (minutes)	Maximum Total Exposure Duration for any 24 hour period (minutes)
1.6	45	150
1.5	120	180
1.4	150	180
1.3	180	210
1.2	210	240
1.1	240	270
1.0	300	300
0.9	360	360
0.8	450	450
0.7	570	570
0.6	720	720

There is no single industry standard for oxygen exposure in recreational nitrox diving. The various training, safety and certification agencies have each adopted a slightly different philosophy regarding the problem, and have proposed or established different exposure limits for open-circuit nitrox diving.

DAN's Research Director, Richard Vann, Ph.D. proposed the most conservative limit of 1.2 ATA in a paper on oxygen exposure management. This limit was set intentionally low to provide a safety cushion for inadvertent increases in PO_2 caused by unplanned depth increases.

For dives involving constant PO_2 rebreathers, the U.S. Navy has set a limit of 1.3 ATA, which coincides with the conservative limit predicted by Dr. Harabin. This approach was taken because these rebreathers keep the PO_2 constant at all exercise levels and depths (down to 150 fsw) throughout the mission which may last up to 8 to 12 hours.

NOAA sets a slightly more conservative limit of three hours at 1.3 ATA, but allows exposures up to 1.6 ATA when exposure times are reduced to 45 minutes (see Table 2-3). While these limits are substantially higher than the USN limits, remember that the scientific divers using open circuit scuba never reach the extended bottom times achieved by Navy divers with rebreathers. In addition, typical dive profiles tend to limit or reduce the time during which the divers are subject to the maximum PO_2. The NOAA divers using these mixtures are highly trained, and the dives are conducted under close supervision.

Some certification agencies defer to the NOAA standards for their PO_2 limits. Again, the use of these limits presupposes a relatively short duration for the dives, and that the entire dive will not be made to the limiting depth. IANTD limits oxygen exposure to 1.6 ATA with a limiting dive time of 45 minutes. ANDI has also established a 1.6 ATA limit, and considers the range from 1.45 to 1.6 as a "cautionary zone."

The PADI and SSI recommended limit for recreational nitrox is 1.4 ATA. (Nitrox tables for both agencies include data for 1.5

and 1.6 ATA in shaded "cautionary" columns.) Most experts consider the 1.4 ATA limit safe because the actual time at the maximum PO_2 will be short. Most dive profiles include significant times at depths less than the maximum depth, so it's unlikely that the divers will be exposed to the limiting PO_2 for the duration of the dive. In addition, recreational nitrox divers using open-circuit scuba carry a limited breathing gas supply, and bottom times are thereby limited to much less than the 8 hour exposures considered by the Navy, or even the 3 hour limit set by NOAA.

When it comes to setting time limits for nitrox dives, the NOAA Oxygen Exposure Limits (Table 2-3) are generally considered the standard of the industry. It's important to recognize that the limits in Table 2-3 include both a maximum exposure per dive, AND a 24 hour cumulative limit. Remember that the 24 hour clock runs continuously, and just because a diver wakes up and it's a new day does not mean that he starts with a clean clock. Nitrox divers must be sure to include the prior day's diving when considering their cumulative exposure. This can be important when a morning dive follows afternoon dives and/or night dives on the previous day.

To add a degree of conservatism, recreational nitrox divers are encouraged to increase their surface intervals any time the exposure on a single dive exceeds 50 percent of the NOAA limit. IANTD requires divers to take a mandatory minimum 45 minute surface interval any time the exposure on a single dive is over 50 percent of the NOAA single dive limit. If the exposure on a single dive is over 90 percent of the limit, the diver incurs a mandatory 90 minute surface interval.

2.8 PULMONARY OXTOX LIMITS AND THE OXYGEN CLOCK

As mentioned earlier in this section, prolonged oxygen exposure poses a potential risk of pulmonary oxygen toxicity. This is of particular concern when oxygen is breathed at partial pressures greater than 0.5 ATA for extended periods. So just as we track our cumulative nitrogen exposure for repetitive dives, it can be important to calculate the cumulative oxygen exposure for repetitive nitrox dives.

The concept of the "oxygen clock" is one way to keep track of our long-term exposure and to limit the potential for pulmonary oxygen toxicity. Using this methodology, exposure is quantified in terms of oxygen tolerance units (OTU's). Various researchers have developed equations for calculating OTU's, but these can be cumbersome to apply when planning or logging a dive in the field. A simpler way of tracking our cumulative oxygen exposure in OTU's is the table-based Repex method (Table 2-4, NOAA, 2000). Using the Repex method, divers can calculate their OTU's/minute based on their maximum PO_2 for each dive.

To calculate the OTU exposure, simply read the OTU/minute for the maximum PO_2 of the dive, and multiply that figure by the bottom time in minutes. Exposures for

TABLE 2-4
REPEX OXYGEN EXPOSURE (NOAA, 2000)

PO_2 (ATM)	OTU's per minute
0.50	0.00
0.55	0.15
0.60	0.27
0.65	0.37
0.70	0.47
0.75	0.56
0.80	0.65
0.85	0.74
0.90	0.83
0.95	0.92
1.00	1.00
1.05	1.08
1.10	1.16
1.15	1.24
1.20	1.32
1.25	1.40
1.30	1.48
1.35	1.55
1.40	1.63
1.45	1.70
1.50	1.78
1.55	1.85
1.60	1.92

TABLE 2-5
MAXIMUM OXYGEN EXPOSURE LIMITS FOR PULMONARY OXYGEN TOXICITY
(NOAA, 2000)

Period (Days)	Maximum Daily Dose (OTU)	Total Exposure (OTU)
1	850	850
2	700	1400
3	620	1860
4	420	2100
5	380	2300
6	350	2520
7	330	2660

repetitive dives over multiple days can be added to obtain the total oxygen exposure. (see Chapter 3 for examples) The maximum exposure limits for pulmonary oxtox are given in Table 2-5 above.

Note that Table 2-5 includes both a maximum daily exposure limit, as well as a cumulative exposure. When making multiple dives over a period of days, the per day limit is reduced substantially. For a single day of diving, the limit is 850 OTU's. If you plan to dive for four consecutive days, the per day limit is reduced to 450 OTU's.

Pulmonary oxygen toxicity is generally considered to be of little concern to typical recreational nitrox divers using open-circuit scuba. Since a diver (or instructor) using nitrox on an extended dive trip making multiple dives per day for several days isn't likely to approach the exposure limits. (See Chapter 3 for examples 17 and 18) However, there is still some evidence that minor symptoms could develop, so divers are encouraged to closely monitor oxygen exposure especially when making multi-day repetitive nitrox dives.

CHAPTER 3

Nitrox Dive Planning

Any nitrox dive requires divers to consider several additional factors beyond those considered for an air dive. First is the maximum partial pressure of oxygen (PO_2max) to be used on the dive. The proper PO_2max must be selected to minimize the risk of oxtox. Given the selected PO_2, plus the depth and bottom time of the dive, the nitrox diver can determine the proper nitrox mixture to use, or determine whether or not the available nitrox mixture is appropriate for the dive under consideration.

There are three primary ways of planning a nitrox dive. The first is what we refer to as the "table based" method. By using tables, divers free themselves from the burden of mathematical computations and the potential errors in calculations.

The second way of planning a nitrox dive is to do the math. It's a little more complex, but it offers the advantage of allowing you to tailor the risk factors — kind of like packing your own parachute for a skydive. Of course, if you haven't been trained, you probably shouldn't pack your own parachute, either.

The third method is to use the planning functions of a nitrox dive computer. The use of nitrox computers will be discussed briefly in Chapter 5.

Regardless of whether you follow the tables or do the math, several elements are absolutely essential to planning a safe recreational nitrox dive, and there are several approaches to determining the proper nitrox mixture or depth and time limits. We'll begin by reviewing the selection of a maximum PO_2. Next, we'll map out the procedures required to determine an appropriate mixture to use for a particular dive. Then we will review the process followed to determine the depth and time limits to be used with a given nitrox mixture (i.e. we already have a cylinder mixed, and now we want to plan our dive around the cylinder of nitrox we have.) Finally, we'll discuss repetitive dives and multiple nitrox mixtures.

3.1 BASIC STEPS IN PLANNING A NITROX DIVE

The basic steps in planning a nitrox dive are:

1. Select the PO_2 limits for the dive based on the depth or the planned bottom time, along with any predisposing factors we may wish to consider.

2. Select the best nitrox mixture for the planned depth OR select the maximum operating depth for the nitrox mixture available. If we want to be conservative, we can simply use the nitrox mixture and follow the standard air no decompression limit and repetitive dive tables. If we wish to extend our bottom times or reduce surface intervals, we go on to the next step.

3. Determine the Equivalent Air Depth (EAD) for the nitrox mixture used. Once we have the EAD for the nitrox mixture we will use for the dive, we can use the air tables and the EAD to determine our no decompression limits.

3.2 SELECTING PO_2 LIMITS

The first step in planning a dive is to determine the PO_2 limit to be used. In the previous chapter, we discussed the various aspects of oxtox and reviewed the limits prescribed by various agencies and organizations. When deciding which limit to use, consider any predisposing factors associated with the dive. For example, ask yourself the following questions regarding the dive plan:

- Will I be working hard?
- Is the water cold?
- Will I be making multiple dives?

If the answer to any of these questions is "yes," consider selecting a more conservative PO_2 for your dive. The first two questions are at best subjective determinations. Only you can determine what constitutes working "hard," or what is "cold." While there's no magic formula, some divers decrease the PO_2max by 0.1 ATA for each predisposing factor.

Another way to approach the PO_2 question is by first establishing the maximum bottom time for your dive. The bottom time may be determined by the objective of your dive, or by the gas supply, depth, and breathing rate. Once you know how long the dive will last, you can select a PO_2 that lies well within the maximum single dive exposure limits.

3.3 DETERMINING THE "BEST MIX"

Once we've determined the maximum depth and the PO_2 for the dive, the next step is to determine the "Best Mix" for the dive. The "Best Mix" is the nitrox mixture that results in the limiting PO_2 at the maximum planned depth. The Best Mix can be determined using Table 3-1.

Example 1:

Let's assume you've selected a PO_2 of 1.3 for a dive to 80 feet. Enter Table 3-1 from the left column (depth) at 80 feet, then read

Table 3-1
Best Mix Recreational Nitrox (EAN)

PO₂ Max (ATA)	1.0	1.1	1.2	1.3	1.4	1.5	1.6
Depth (fsw)							
10	40	40	40	40	40	40	40
20	40	40	40	40	40	40	40
30	40	40	40	40	40	40	40
40	38	40	40	40	40	40	40
50	36	40	40	40	40	40	40
60	34	38	40	40	40	40	40
70	32	34	38	40	40	40	40
80	30	32	34	36	40	40	40
90	28	30	32	34	36	40	40
100	24	28	30	32	34	36	38
110			28	30	32	34	36
120			24	28	30	32	34
130					28	30	32
50% CNS Limit-Min (45 min SI Req.)	150	120	105	90	75	60	22
90% CNS Limit-Min (2 hour SI Req.)	270	216	189	162	135	108	40
100% CNS Limit-Min	300	240	210	180	150	120	45

Low Risk Caution Range Danger Zone

the Best Mix EAN under the column marked 1.3. In this case, the Best Mix is EAN 36, or 36% oxygen. Using EAN 36 on a dive to 80 feet will result in a PO_2 of 1.3 at that depth.

Example 2:

Assume we're planning a dive to 80 feet with a PO_2 of 1.6 ATA. In this case, we also enter Table 3-1 at the 80 foot level in the left column. Reading across to the 1.6 column, the table lists EAN 40 as the Best mix. (Note: In this case, the theoretical Best Mix would actually be 47%, but in recreational nitrox we are limited to a maximum of 40% oxygen, hence the value of EAN 40.)

Example 3:

Now, let's assume we're planning a dive to 100 feet using a PO_2 limit of 1.3. We enter Table 3-1 at the 100 foot level and read across to the 1.3ATA column. The table lists EAN 32 for this dive.

We can also calculate the Best Mix nitrox mixture for the dive using the following equation (oxygen "T"):

$$\frac{PO_2}{FO_2 \mid PT}$$

Where: PO_2 = oxygen partial pressure in ATA
FO_2 = the fraction of oxygen in the mixture, and
P T = the total pressure in ATA at the maximum depth
Note: To use the Oxygen T, the top number (PO_2) is product of the bottom two numbers (FO_2 x PT). Divide PO_2 by FO_2 to get PT, or Divide PO_2 by PT to get FO_2.

In this example, we first convert 100 feet to total pressure in ATA using the equation:

$(D/33) + 1 = ATA$, or in this case
$(100/33) + 1 = 4.03$ ATA

Next, we calculate the best mix using the oxygen "T" as follows:

$$\frac{PO_2}{FO_2 \mid PT}$$

Substituting in the oxygen "T" yields

$$\frac{1.3}{FO_2 \mid 4.03}$$

Dividing 1.3 by 4.03, we get:

$FO_2 = 0.32$, or EAN 32, which is the same answer we got using Table 3-1.

Example 4:

Assume you plan to dive to 80 feet, and have decided to use the standard NOAA PO_2 limit of 1.6 ATA. First, convert 80 feet to the equivalent pressure in ATA using the equation:

$(D/33) + 1 = ATA$, or in this case
$(80/33) + 1 = 3.42$ ATA

Substituting these values in the oxygen T, we get:

$$\frac{1.6}{FO_2 \mid 3.42}$$

Dividing 1.6 by 3.42, we get:

$FO_2 = 0.47$

So, the highest acceptable mixture in terms of single-dive oxygen toxicity, is EAN 47. Since recreational nitrox limits us to EAN 40, that might be our choice for the dive.

Example 5:

Assume we are planning repetitive, arduous dives in cold water to a depth of 100 feet. If we normally choose a PO_2max of 1.6 ATA, we might decide to reduce the PO_2max for each of the three disposing factors (repetitive, cold, and hard work), yielding a 1.3 ATA limit for this dive. We first convert 100 feet to ATA:

(D/33) +1 = ATA, or in this case
(100/33) + 1 = 4.03 ATA

Substituting these values in the oxygen T, we get:

$$\frac{1.3}{FO_2 \mid 4.03}$$

$FO_2 = 0.32$

So, the highest acceptable mixture, in terms of single-dive oxygen toxicity, is EAN 32.

Example 6:

Now we're planning a dive to 60 feet. We know the water will be cold and we'll be working hard, so we want to be very conservative. We start with the recommended limit of 1.4 ATA, and reduce this value for our predisposing factors. This gives us a 1.2 ATA limit for this dive. We first convert 60 feet to ATA:

$(D/33) + 1 = ATA$, or in this case
$(60/33) + 1 = 2.82$ ATA

Substituting these values in the oxygen T, we get:

$$\frac{1.2}{FO_2 \mid 2.82}$$

$FO_2 = 0.43$

So, the highest acceptable mixture for this dive, in terms of single-dive oxygen toxicity, is EAN 43. Since recreational nitrox limits us to EAN 40, that might be our choice for this dive.

3.4 MAXIMUM OPERATING DEPTH

Sometimes we only have a particular nitrox blend available to us, so we must plan our dive around the available gas. In this case, we want to determine the maximum depth we can dive using that blend. This limit is referred to as the Maximum Operating Depth or MOD. Given the limiting PO_2 for the particular dive, we can determine the MOD using Table 3-2.

Example 7:

Assume we have EAN 36 available and we are planning a drift dive in warm water. We expect this to be an easy, low-stress dive, so we don't add any additional conservatism. Using the PADI limit, we choose 1.4 ATA as our limiting PO_2. We enter the left column at the EAN value of 36, and read across to the column marked 1.4 ATA. The table gives us a MOD of 95 feet. If we dive deeper than 95 feet with EAN 36, we will exceed a PO_2 of 1.4 ATA.

TABLE 3-2
MOD (FSW) FOR RECREATIONAL NITROX

PO₂ Max (ATA)	1.0	1.1	1.2	1.3	1.4	1.5	1.6
EAN							
24	130+	130+	130+	130+	130+	130+	130+
26	130+	130+	130+	130+	130+	130+	130+
28	130+	130+	130+	120	130+	130+	130+
30	130+	130+	130+	110	121	130+	130+
32	130+	130+	130+	101	111	122	130+
34	130+	130+	130+	93	103	113	122
36	130+	130+	130+	86	95	105	114
38	130+	130+	130+	80	89	97	106
40	130+	130+	130+	74	82	91	99
50% CNS Limit-Min (45 min SI Req.)	150	120	105	90	75	60	22
90% CNS Limit-Min (2 hour SI Req.)	270	216	189	162	135	108	40
100% CNS Limit-Min	300	240	210	130	160	120	45
Low Risk — Normal Operations		Caution Range					Danger: 1.6 ATA PO₂

Note: MODs exceeding the 130 foot recreational diving depth limit are listed as 130+.

NITROX DIVE PLANNING

Example 8:

Let's say we're making the same dive as in Example 7 above, but choose a less conservative PO_2 of 1.6 ATA. In this example, we enter Table 3-2 under EAN 36 and read across to the 1.6 ATA column. The MOD listed is 114 feet.

Example 9:

Assume we're diving with EAN 30 and choose a PO_2 of 1.3ATA. We enter the left column under EAN 30 and read across to the 1.3 column to find the MOD of 110 feet.

3.5 EQUIVALENT AIR DEPTH

The next step in the planning process is determining the equivalent air depth (EAD) for the nitrox mixture selected. The EAD is the depth where the partial pressure of nitrogen in air equals the partial pressure of nitrogen in the nitrox blend at the actual depth. Or to put it in simple terms, the EAD is the depth at which our body "thinks" it is diving with respect to nitrogen absorption. We can determine the EAD for any recreational nitrox mixture using Table 3-3. Enter the left column under the nitrox mixture being used (round DOWN to the next lower mixture if your mixture is between listed values), read across to the actual depth to which you will be diving, and read the EAD.

Example 10:

We are using EAN 30 and plan to dive to 100 feet. We enter Table 3-3 in the left column under EAN 30, and read the EAD of 85 feet under the column marked 100 feet. So when diving at 100 feet using EAN 30, we absorb nitrogen as if we were breathing air at 85 feet. Using no-decompression air tables to determine our maximum bottom time, we select the 85 foot table (or round to 90 feet).

Table 3-3
EAD for Recreational Nitrox Mixtures

Actual Depth (fsw) EAN	40	50	60	70	80	90	100	110	120	130
24	37	47	56	66	76	85	95	105	114	124
26	35	45	54	63	73	82	92	101	110	120
28	34	43	52	61	70	79	88	97	106	116
30	32	41	49	58	67	76	85	94	103	111
32	30	38	47	56	64	73	81	90	99	107
34	28	36	45	53	61	70	78	86	95	
36	26	34	42	50	59	67	75	83		
38	24	32	40	48	56	64	71			
40	22	30	38	45	53	60	66			

Low Risk

Caution Range
$PO_2 > 1.4$ ATA

Danger Zone
$PO_2 \geq 1.6$ ATA

Example 11:

In this example, let's assume we're using EAN 38 and plan a dive to 90 feet. We enter Table 3-3 in the left column under 38, and read across to our depth of 90 feet. The table yields an EAD of 64 feet. This area of the table is shaded, indicating a PO_2 in excess of 1.4 ATA but below 1.6 ATA. While diving with EAN 38 at 90 feet, our body absorbs nitrogen at the same rate as if we were breathing air at 64 feet. We can use a 65 foot air table (or round to 70 feet) to determine our NDL.

Example 12:

Now we're planning a dive with EAN 38 to 70 feet. We enter Table 3-3 in the left column under 38, and read across to our depth of 70 feet. The table yields an EAD of 48 feet. While diving with EAN 38 at 70 feet, our body absorbs nitrogen at the same rate as if we were breathing air at 48 feet. We can use a 50 foot air table to determine our NDL.

We can also determine the EAD mathematically using the equation:

$$EAD = [(FN_2 \times (D + 33))/.79] - 33$$

Where: EAD = Equivalent Air Depth in Feet
FN_2 = The fraction of gas which is nitrogen
(or 1 - oxygen fraction)
D = Depth in Feet of the actual dive

Substituting the values, we get:
$FN_2 = 1 - 0.38 = 0.62$
$EAD = [(0.62 \times (70 + 33))/.79] - 33$
$EAD = 47.8$ feet, the same answer given in Table 3-3

Example 13:

Let's assume we're using EAN 36 (36% oxygen) at a depth of 80 feet. Remember that the nitrogen fraction is 1 minus the oxygen fraction, or .64 in this case. Substituting the values into the above equation, we get:

$$EAD = [(0.64 \times (80 + 33))/.79] - 33$$
$$= 58.5 \text{ feet}$$

In other words, the nitrogen uptake on a dive to 80 feet on EAN 36 is equivalent to a dive to 58.5 feet breathing air. We round this up to 60 feet and go to our standard air dive tables to calculate our NDL for this dive.

Example 14:

Assume we're using EAN 40 on a dive to 60 feet. Substituting the values into the EAD equation, we get:

$$EAD = [(0.60 \times (60 + 33))/.79] - 33$$
$$= 37.6 \text{ feet}$$

Breathing EAN 40 at a depth of 60 feet, we absorb nitrogen at the same rate as breathing air at 37.6 feet. We round up to the deeper depth and use the 40 foot air table to calculate our NDL.

Example 15:

In this example, let's assume we're using EAN 30 at a depth of 100 feet. Substituting the values into the EAD equation, we get:

$$EAD = [(0.70 \times (100 + 33))/.79] - 33$$
$$= 84.8 \text{ feet}$$

Breathing EAN 30 at a depth of 100 feet, we absorb nitrogen at the same rate as breathing air at 84.8 feet. We round up to the deeper depth and use either an 85 foot or 90 foot air table to calculate our NDL.

3.6 CUMULATIVE OXYGEN EXPOSURE

To further limit the potential for CNS oxygen toxicity, we must also limit our exposure on a single dive to no more than the NOAA Single Exposure Limit for the PO_2 limit selected (see Table 2-3). The exposure can be calculated using the following formula:

$$CNS\% = (ABT \times 100)/(MEL)$$

Where: ABT = Actual Bottom Time
MEL = Maximum Exposure Limit (NOAA Single Dive Exposure Limit)

If our CNS% exceeds 50% on any dive, we incur a mandatory 45 minute surface interval before making a repetitive dive. If we meet the 90% CNS on any dive, we incur a mandatory 2 hour surface interval before making a repetitive dive. We must never exceed the 100% CNS limit in any 24 hour period. These limits are listed on Tables 3-1 and 3-2.

As mentioned earlier in this chapter, another approach to planning a nitrox dive is to select a PO_2 based on our planned bottom time and depth.

Example 16:

Assume you plan to do some underwater photography at a depth of 90 feet and plan to stay there for a bottom time of 60 minutes.

Table 3-3 gives us an EAD of 60 feet for this depth with EAN 40, and our NDL (based on the U.S. Navy Tables) is 60 minutes. Table 3-2 tells us we can dive to 90 feet on EAN 40 without exceeding a PO_2 of 1.5 ATA, but our oxygen exposure is 50% of the CNS limit. Thus, we incur a mandatory 45 minute surface interval following this dive.

Cumulative oxygen exposure can also be calculated in terms of the oxygen clock or Repex method described in Chapter 2. As the following examples illustrate, the risk of pulmonary or "whole body" oxtox is very low for recreational nitrox diving. However, symptoms of pulmonary oxtox have been reported in divers breathing high oxygen mixes for long periods over several days. Divers, guides, and instructors who routinely make repetitive dives on nitrox may be at a slightly higher risk of pulmonary oxtox.

Example 17:

Assume a diver makes a 45 minute dive to 80 feet on EAN 38. From Table 3-2, we find his PO_2 is 1.3 ATA. His oxygen exposure for this dive can be calculated by multiplying the corresponding OTU/minute of 1.48 times 45 minutes (from Table 2-4, Repex Oxygen Exposure). This yields an oxygen exposure of 66.6 OTU's for the dive. If three such dives are made in a day, the cumulative exposure is the sum of the three dives, or 199.8 OTUs for the day, well below the 850 OTU single day limit, and below the 330 OTU daily limit for 7-days of diving (Table 2-5).

Example 18:

Let's assume a diver uses EAN 40 for a dive to 100 feet. His PO_2 is 1.6 ATA (from Table 3-2), and the corresponding exposure rate is 1.92 OTU per minute (Table 2-4). The diver's EAD is 68 feet (Table 3-3), so we round up to 70, and from the U.S. Navy Air No-Decompression Tables we determine the NDL to be 50 minutes. If the diver has a 45 minute bottom time, his oxygen exposure for the dive is 1.92 x 45 or 86.4 OTUs. Three such dives in a day add up to 259.2 OTUs for the day. Even after a week of repetitive exposures, the daily exposure is less than the 330 OTU/day limit, and the cumulative exposure is about 1,814, or about 70% of the 2660 OTU exposure limit of Table 2-5.

Due to the low risk of pulmonary oxtox in recreational nitrox diving, some agencies and instructors have attempted to simplify the cumulative oxygen exposure tracking. For example, SSI limits all dives to EAN 36 or lower, and sets a maximum PO_2 limit of 1.4 ATA. As long as divers follow these limits, and restrict their dives to the NOAA limits of 150 minutes of bottom time per dive and 180 minutes of bottom time per day, the divers are relieved of the need to track cumulative oxygen exposure.

3.7 REPETITIVE DIVES

Making repetitive dives on nitrox is no different than making repetitive dives on compressed air. All we must do is follow the air tables using the actual depths (more conservative) or the appropriate EAD. The same criteria and safe diving practices we apply to air diving also apply to nitrox. This means deeper dives should be made prior to shallower dives. In keeping with this philosophy, the EAD for the first dives should be greater than those for subsequent dives. While some speculate that reverse profiles (deep dives following shallow dives) do not pose a problem when a computer is used rather than dive tables, the mechanism of DCI are not well enough understood, nor has adequate research been conducted to prove the safety of reverse profiles. Until such research has been completed and the results verified, divers should adhere to the long-held practice of conducting deeper dives prior to shallow dives.

Often times divers will want to use different mixtures for repetitive dives. This is a generally accepted procedure in recreational nitrox diving. Divers can readily change nitrox mixtures for different repetitive dives, or even use air for some dives. However, it is recommended that divers use the mixture that provides the deeper EAD on the first dive.

3.8 CHOOSING DIVE TABLES

In today's world of diving there are many choices. Among these is a choice of which dive tables to use. Depending on your training and certification, you may be more comfortable using one set of tables over another. However, there are some important points you should consider when making this most important choice.

The U.S. Navy Air No-Decompression Tables have long been used for nitrox diving and have a well-established safety record. Technical divers often favor the Navy tables since the model used to develop them includes a 120 minute tissue, making them appropriate for decompression diving. The PADI Recreational Dive Planner has more conservative no-decompression limits, however its slowest tissue is a 60 minute tissue. As a result, it provides reduced surface intervals, but is inappropriate for decompression diving.

The model used to develop the DCIEM tables uses serial rather than parallel tissue compartments, and is considered by some to be a more appropriate model for gas diffusion in human tissues. These tables have also been tested extensively by wet divers in cold (40 to 50°F) water, and have an excellent safety record.

NOAA publishes tables for use with its standard mixtures (NN32 and NN36). These have been used successfully for decades and are very easy to use.

Remember that no dive table can prevent all occurrences of DCI. When choosing a dive table for nitrox diving, follow the recommendations of your nitrox certification agency, and then follow established conservative diving protocols.

Notes

CHAPTER 4

Equipment Requirements

A common question posed by prospective nitrox divers revolves around the need for special equipment. As explained in Chapter One, relatively little specialized equipment is needed for recreational nitrox diving. For the most part, the same equipment used for recreational air diving can be used for nitrox diving, as long as we don't use mixtures greater than 40% oxygen (the limit for recreational nitrox diving). However, the increased fraction of oxygen in nitrox may cause an increased rate of oxidation and deterioration of O-rings, seals and other components compared to use with clean, compressed air. Some manufacturers provide "nitrox compatible" equipment in which different O-ring, seal, and lubricant materials have been installed to slow the deteriorating oxidation process.

Most regulators, BC's, and instrument consoles are generally compatible with recreational nitrox mixtures. Even a dive computer designed for use with air can usually be used if a diver chooses not to extend his bottom times when using nitrox. Before using any equipment such as regulators, BC's, instruments and computers with nitrox, check with the manufacturer or dive equipment technician.

If we use a dive computer, and dive with nitrox to provide a safety margin against DCS, then we can simply use the same computer we use for air dives and limit our depths to the MOD for the nitrox mixture being used. The only drawback to using the air computer is that it will not warn us as we approach oxtox limits — a typical feature of computers designed for nitrox. If we plan to take full advantage of the extended bottom times afforded by nitrox, we'll need to revert to table-based diving, or use a dive computer designed for use with nitrox.

4.1 NITROX CYLINDERS

If a cylinder is to be used for nitrox diving, it must be properly labeled according to industry standards. If a cylinder will be filled using the partial pressure blending technique (see Chapter 6), it will be exposed to hazardous oxygen concentrations during the process, and therefore must be appropriately oxygen-cleaned. The need for oxygen cleaning a nitrox cylinder stems from the potential explosion risk when exposed to high concentrations of oxygen, especially at high pressures. An oxygen clean nitrox cylinder will bear a sticker indicating that it has been oxygen cleaned. Oxygen cleaning of cylinders is required any time potential contamination occurs (such as being filled with regular compressed breathing air), or on an annual basis.

The process of oxygen cleaning is designed to remove any contaminants, particularly hydrocarbons, which may spontaneously ignite when exposed to high concentrations of oxygen. This includes silicone grease and other lubricants normally used in the cylinder valves. In addition, O-rings and other components may require replacement with those made from oxygen compatible materials. Since most divers rent their cylinders, the need for a nitrox cylinder becomes a moot point.

Labeling is necessary to insure that divers planning air dives do not use cylinders charged with nitrox. (see Chapter 5) A technician will not fill a cylinder with nitrox unless it bears the proper nitrox label.

4.2 OXYGEN ANALYZERS

Probably the most important equipment for a recreational nitrox diver is an oxygen analyzer. It is absolutely imperative that a diver knows the oxygen content of a cylinder before entering the water and beginning a dive. (see Chapter 5) Failure to check the oxygen content of a cylinder can lead to serious injuries such as decompression illness, or even death if an oxygen toxicity convulsion occurs during the dive.

In recent years, numerous manufacturers have developed inexpensive and reliable oxygen analyzers designed for analyzing nitrox mixtures. Procedures for calibrating and using oxygen analyzers vary from one manufacturer to another, as does the shelf life and operating life of the sensors. Before using an oxygen analyzer, a diver must verify that it is within calibration limits, and be familiar with its operating procedures.

4.3 NITROX COMPUTERS

A nitrox computer eliminates much of the table work, but some additional steps and crosschecks are required. Since nitrox can be mixed in virtually any proportion, it's imperative that we program our computer for the mixture we're using. Most models allow divers to select the maximum PO_2 for the dive, and provide alarms when this limit is approached. Additional parameters such as altitude, type of dive (strenuous, cold, or normal) and other personal safety factors may also be required input. Inputting these parameters can alter the algorithm to provide an additional degree of conservatism. Many models, in addition to the max PO_2 alarm, have an oxygen clock function to track CNS% and pulmonary oxygen toxicity exposure.

While it is beyond the scope of this book to provide a detailed comparison of nitrox computers, suffice it to say that there are significant differences in the algorithms (mathematical models) used to determine no-decompression limits for the various nitrox computers available on today's market. Unless a diver has been specifically trained in decompression diving and is fully aware of the operational limits and constraints inherent in a computer's design, he should not attempt decompression diving with nitrox.

While modern nitrox computers are endowed with a myriad of features, perhaps the most important are the planning functions. These features can help greatly in determining limits and constraints for repetitive and multi-day nitrox diving. However, the user must be fully knowledgeable of the planning functions before attempting to plan a nitrox dive. Remember too that safe diving protocol applies to all forms of recreational diving, regardless of what a dive computer might allow.

The most important aspect of using a nitrox computer is that the proper information be accurately programmed prior to diving. If the computer is programmed for a nitrox blend other than the one used by the diver, the results could be serious injury or death. Never use a nitrox computer without the proper training, and follow the manufacturer's operating and maintenance instructions carefully.

Several important points should be kept in mind when choosing a nitrox computer. First, the computer should have an easy-to-see and easily understood screen(s) that works well throughout the range of lighting including night dives. Required programming should be simple to accomplish, with default parameters that minimize risk. For many users, a PC interface is an important feature, allowing dive data to be downloaded for evaluation and dive logging. The user manual should be thorough, complete, and easy to understand. If possible, test dive several nitrox computers before making your final decision.

CHAPTER 5

Procedures and Safeguards

Considering the potential risk of injury with the misuse of nitrox mixtures, it is essential that the proper procedures and safeguards be taken when obtaining nitrox fills and before diving with a cylinder of nitrox. These procedures and safeguards pertain in particular to the labeling of nitrox cylinders, verification of nitrox mixtures, and the appropriate record keeping for the nitrox fill station. As a further safeguard, nitrox divers must always be on the lookout for symptoms of oxygen toxicity, and be prepared to take the appropriate action should symptoms develop during a dive.

5.1 NITROX CYLINDER LABELING

It is absolutely essential that cylinders used for nitrox be properly labeled. Before a cylinder is filled, the technician at the fill station may require assurance that the cylinder is oxygen-clean and compatible with the mixing technique to be used to prepare the nitrox mix. In addition, the mixtures contained in nitrox cylinders can be dangerous or even lethal to those not trained in nitrox diving. So, it is critically important to have all nitrox cylinders appropriately identified.

Standard labeling for nitrox cylinders makes them easily identifiable, both to nitrox divers and those not trained in nitrox diving. The marking consists of a 4-inch green band with wording to indicate a nitrox mixture ("Nitrox," "Nitrox Only," "Enriched Air," "Enriched Air Nitrox"). The green band is bordered both top and bottom with a 1-inch yellow band. An alternative nitrox label is a yellow cylinder with a 4-inch green band with wording to indicate nitrox.

Figure 5-1 Labeling of nitrox cylinders makes them readily identifiable even to non-nitrox divers.

Figure 5-2 An Oxygen Service Label identifies a cylinder as "oxygen clean" and identifies the limits of its use.

Figure 5-3 A contents tag or sticker on a nitrox cylinder identifies the components of the breathing gas.

PROCEDURES AND SAFEGUARDS

In addition to the primary nitrox label, a nitrox cylinder may also carry two additional labels. One is a label that identifies the limits of its use with oxygen. An "oxygen service rating" denoting that the cylinder has been "oxygen-cleaned" and is oxygen compatible is required if the cylinder will be exposed to more than 40% oxygen during the filling process, such as during partial pressure blending. (see Chapter 6) A cylinder may also carry a specific label or contents tag to identify the contents (mixture) contained by the cylinder.

***Note**: Never fill an oxygen-clean cylinder with standard compressed air. Doing so may contaminate the cylinder, causing an explosion risk when the cylinder is again filled with nitrox. If an oxygen-clean cylinder is inadvertently filled with standard breathing air, it should be so noted, and the cylinder appropriately cleaned prior to being entered into oxygen service again.

5.2 VERIFYING THE MIXTURE

Perhaps the most critical step in nitrox diving is verification of the mixture in the scuba cylinder. All nitrox divers are trained to personally test every nitrox tank to verify the proper mix before it is used. If you follow a nitrox table on a dive while inadvertently using air, you're likely to suffer a serious case of DCI. Likewise, following a deep air-dive profile with a strong blend of nitrox could result in a fatal case of oxygen toxicity.

The verification testing of a nitrox cylinder is performed before accepting the cylinder at the fill station using a commercially available oxygen monitor. The verification testing is either accomplished by the diver himself, or by a technician under the supervision of the diver. For a proper reading, make certain that the filling manifold is detached from the cylinder. The blend should be within 1% of the requested oxygen fraction, otherwise a new MOD and EAD must be determined prior to using the cylinder.

Figure 5-4
A diver verifies the oxygen content of a nitrox cylinder after receiving a fill.

After calibrating the monitor, test the contents of the cylinder and mark the cylinder (use a grease pencil or marker), placard, or contents tag indicating your name and the percent oxygen. Some divers also write the MOD on the cylinder or placard, but remember that the MOD changes depending on the PO_2max selected. Don't fall into the trap of diving with a cylinder of nitrox to a depth that someone else considered safe. Some agencies also require that the diver record the fill date on the cylinder, along with the name or initials of the person performing the gas analysis.

Finally, many dive centers and fill stations require each diver receiving a nitrox fill to sign a form that records the serial number of the cylinder and the percent oxygen. Divers should reverify the contents immediately prior to the dive. This is especially critical if the cylinder has been out of their direct control at any time since the cylinder was filled.

5.3 RECORD KEEPING

Operators providing nitrox are generally required by their certification agencies to keep careful records of nitrox fills. Divers receiving nitrox fills are usually required to sign a release to limit the liability of the operator. The exact data required varies from one operator to another depending on the certification agency requirements. However, a diver receiving the nitrox fill typically must verify that the proper cylinder was filled, that the mixture was tested and found within the proper limits, and that the recipient of the cylinder was a certificated nitrox diver. If a problem is detected with the fill station, such records may be helpful in tracking the affected cylinders and divers.

5.4 RECOGNIZING OXTOX SYMPTOMS

Although proper planning should prevent its occurrence, nitrox divers must learn to recognize the symptoms of oxygen toxicity. A mnemonic taught by many instructors to remember the symptoms is ConVENTID. The letters stand for eight common symptoms of CNS toxicity:

- Convulsions (the most critical, life-threatening symptom)
- Visual disturbances including blurred and tunnel vision
- Ear or hearing abnormalities such as ringing (tinnitus) and roaring
- Nausea and vomiting
- Twitching or Tingling sensations, especially of the face and lips
- Irritability or Irrationality
- Dizziness or Vertigo

A more convenient mnemonic for remembering the symptoms comes from rearranging the letters as I-C-D EVENT, which also incorporates a second E for the feelings of Euphoria that can accompany oxygen toxicity.

If any of these symptoms are detected during a nitrox dive, the affected diver and his buddy should ascend immediately.

5.5 EMERGENCY ACTION FOR OXTOX CONVULSIONS

If a diver experiences an oxtox convulsion, chances are he will spit out his regulator and drown unless a buddy or rescue diver gives immediate assistance. The U.S. Navy Diving Manual recommends the following actions to assist a convulsing diver:

a. Assume a position behind the convulsing diver. Release the victim's weight belt unless he is wearing a drysuit, in which case the weight belt should be left in place to prevent the diver from assuming a face down position on the surface.
b. Leave the victim's mouthpiece in his mouth. If it is not in his mouth, do not attempt to replace it.
c. Grasp the victim around his chest above the underwater breathing apparatus (UBA) or between the UBA and his body. If difficulty is encountered in gaining control of the

victim in this manner, the rescuer should use the best method possible to gain control. The UBA waist or neck strap may be grasped if necessary.
  d. Make a controlled ascent to the surface, maintaining a slight pressure on the diver's chest to assist exhalation.
  e. If additional buoyancy is required, activate the victim's (buoyancy compensator). The rescuer should not release his own weight belt or inflate his own (buoyancy compensator).
  f. Upon reaching the surface, inflate the victim's (buoyancy compensator) if not previously done.
  g. Remove the victim's mouthpiece (after the victim is no longer actively convulsing).
  h. Signal for emergency pick-up.
  i. Once the convulsion has subsided, open the victim's airway by tilting his head back slightly.
  j. Ensure the victim is breathing. Mouth-to-mouth breathing may be initiated if necessary.
  k. If an upward excursion occurred during the actual convulsion, transport to the nearest (recompression) chamber and have the victim evaluated by an individual trained to treat diving-related illness.

***Note**: Although an ascent to the surface could result in arterial gas embolism, this is generally considered a better option than keeping a convulsing victim underwater where drowning is highly probable. The primary objective is to prevent the victim from drowning. Also, look for foreign bodies, such as mouthpiece bite tabs, which may have been bitten off during the convulsion in the trachea, which could block the victim's airway.

CHAPTER 6

How Nitrox Is Made

Although the means by which nitrox is prepared is virtually transparent to the diver, a basic understanding of the processes available lends important insights for the recreational nitrox diver.

6.1 OXYGEN HANDLING HAZARDS

The primary danger or hazard in preparation of nitrox is the fire/explosion risk involved with handling oxygen. Any equipment that will be exposed to greater than 40 percent oxygen must be properly oxygen cleaned to remove contaminants that can spontaneously ignite when exposed to high concentrations of oxygen.

Likewise, air that will be mixed with greater than 40 percent oxygen must be "oxygen compatible." Even low levels of contaminants such as condensed hydrocarbon (oil) droplets found in normal compressed breathing air can accumulate over time resulting in an explosion hazard. Tiny particles of rust and other debris ricocheting around pipes and fittings can generate enough of a spark to ignite an oxygen-rich mixture.

The industry standard for air used in scuba diving is the CGA (Compressed Gas Association) Grade E breathing air (see Table 6-1). Although this air is safe from a human physiological standpoint,

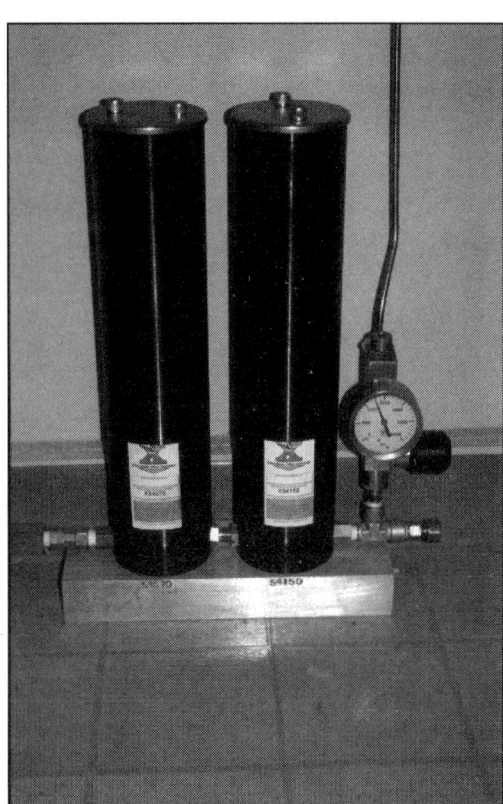

**Figure 6-1
A hyperfiltration system is used to produce oxygen compatible air.**

TABLE 6-1
BREATHING AIR STANDARDS

Contaminant	CGA Grade E Limit	Modified CGA Grade E (O_2 Compatible) Limit
Carbon Monoxide	10 ppm	2 ppm
Carbon Dioxide	1,000 ppm	1,000 ppm
Oil and Particles	5 mg/cubic meter	0.1 mg/cubic meter
Water Vapor	67 ppm (-50° F dewpoint)	67 ppm (-50° F dewpoint)

additional filtration is required to remove trace levels of hydrocarbons and other contaminants before Grade E air can be safely mixed with pure oxygen.

The process by which the oxygen compatible Modified Grade E air is made is referred to as hyperfiltration. The hyperfiltration process is designed to remove trace amounts of contaminants, especially oil and other hydrocarbons, and to filter out particles as small as 2 microns in diameter. A typical hyperfilter uses a blend of high-grade activated carbons and other adsorbents to reduce hydrocarbons to the 0.1 mg/cubic meter limit. A high quality hyperfiltration system is designed to control the flow through the filter media to ensure adequate dwell times, or contact time between filtration media and contaminants, to ensure proper filtration. The filter beds are also sized to accommodate fluctuations in compressor performance that may result in below standard quality inlet air.

6.2 PARTIAL PRESSURE BLENDING

Probably the most straightforward process by which nitrox is mixed is called partial pressure blending. Because it involves the use of pure oxygen, it is a potentially hazardous operation, and should only be performed by trained technicians using the proper tools, equipment and procedures.

Partial pressure blending is accomplished by first charging a cylinder to a predetermined pressure with pure oxygen. The technician typically uses a set of mixing tables or mathematical equations to determine the required oxygen charge for a particular operating pressure and nitrox blend. Starting with an empty cylinder allows the process to be accomplished with a relatively low-pressure oxygen source, although the process can also be used (and tables are readily available for) partially filled cylinders if the requisite oxygen pressure is available.

After the oxygen is bled into the cylinder, the cylinder is charged to the desired operating pressure with oxygen-compatible

Figure 6-2
A technician uses partial pressure blending to fill a nitrox cylinder.

(modified Grade E) air. Before the nitrox is used, the oxygen content is verified with an oxygen analyzer, and modifications to the gas mixture are made. This technique is used to fill large quantity nitrox storage banks as well as to fill individual scuba cylinders.

Since pure oxygen is used in the process, the equipment used for partial pressure blending must be oxygen-clean. Individual cylinders being filled by this process must also be oxygen clean since they will be exposed to oxygen levels exceeding 40 percent during the process. The air blended with the oxygen must also be oxygen-compatible since it too is mixed with high concentrations of oxygen.

6.3 CONTINUOUS FLOW BLENDING

A second process for preparing nitrox is referred to as continuous flow blending. Developed under the direction of Dr. J. Morgan Wells, Director of NOAA's Diving Program, this process utilizes a precision oxygen injection system to inject high-purity oxygen in the proper proportion with air as it enters an oil-free high-pressure compressor system. As the nitrox blend exits the compressor, the oxygen concentration is analyzed, and a technician makes the necessary adjustments to the oxygen injection system to fine-tune the nitrox blend. As with partial pressure blending, the air to be mixed with the oxygen must be oxygen-compatible.

In the past few years, some new devices have been developed to improve continuous flow blending. One such device called the Nitrox Stik™ uses vane technology to blend air and oxygen. One end of the device is connected to a high or low-pressure oxygen source, and the other to the inlet of a high-pressure air compressor. Air and oxygen are mixed in a highly turbulent flow regime, resulting in well-mixed nitrox blends that can be compressed using an oil-lubricated compressor. The device can also adapt partial-pressure-blending systems to more efficient continuous flow blending with standard air compressors. Manufacturers are also making strides in the automation of continuous flow blending systems to improve efficiency and safety.

6.4 PRESSURE SWING ABSORPTION (PSA)

Pressure swing absorption (PSA) technology utilizes molecular sieves to selectively remove nitrogen from an air stream. The process can generate oxygen with purity of up to 95 percent, and is often used as the source of oxygen for continuous-flow blending. Using PSA to generate nitrox follows a two-step process. The first step is generation of high purity oxygen. The second step is essentially a continuous flow blending process wherein the oxygen is blended with air to produce the desired mix.

The underlying concept behind PSA is the ability of particular materials known as "molecular sieves" to selectively remove nitrogen from an air stream. Variations in pressure determine the amount of nitrogen that can be absorbed by the molecular sieve. A PSA system (Figure 6-3) utilizes two molecular sieve beds operating in parallel, driven by a low-pressure compressor or other inlet air source delivering filtered air at roughly 50 to 90 psig. As one bed is in its pressurization cycle filtering out nitrogen and generating high purity oxygen, the other is in its desaturation or depressurization mode releasing the nitrogen absorbed in the previous cycle. The high purity oxygen exits the bed in the range of roughly 45 to 60 psig. This low-pressure oxygen flows into a receiving tank where pressure fluctuations from the beds are modulated.

Oxygen flowing from the receiving tank passes through a nitrox-blending valve, which mixes the oxygen with ambient air to produce the proper blend of nitrox. The nitrox is then pumped to the desired pressure. Pressures up to 4,500 psig are possible using a water-immersed high-pressure nitrox compressor.

The key to the PSA system is the valve sequencing, which alternates the airflow from one molecular sieve bed to the other at the appropriate time. Mechanical cam-operated systems have been successfully used for decades, but modern PSA systems utilize a microprocessor (programmable logic circuitry, or PLC) to sequence the valves. These systems achieve greater efficiency and higher oxygen purity.

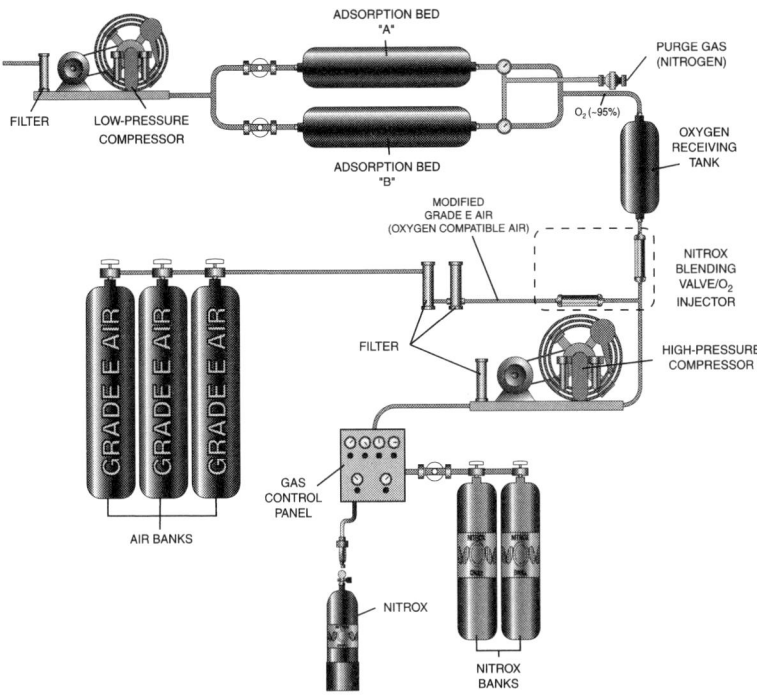

Rick Melvin, DAN
Curt Bowen, Undersea Breathing Systems, Inc.

**Figure 6-3
Typical Pressure Swing Absorption (PSA) System**

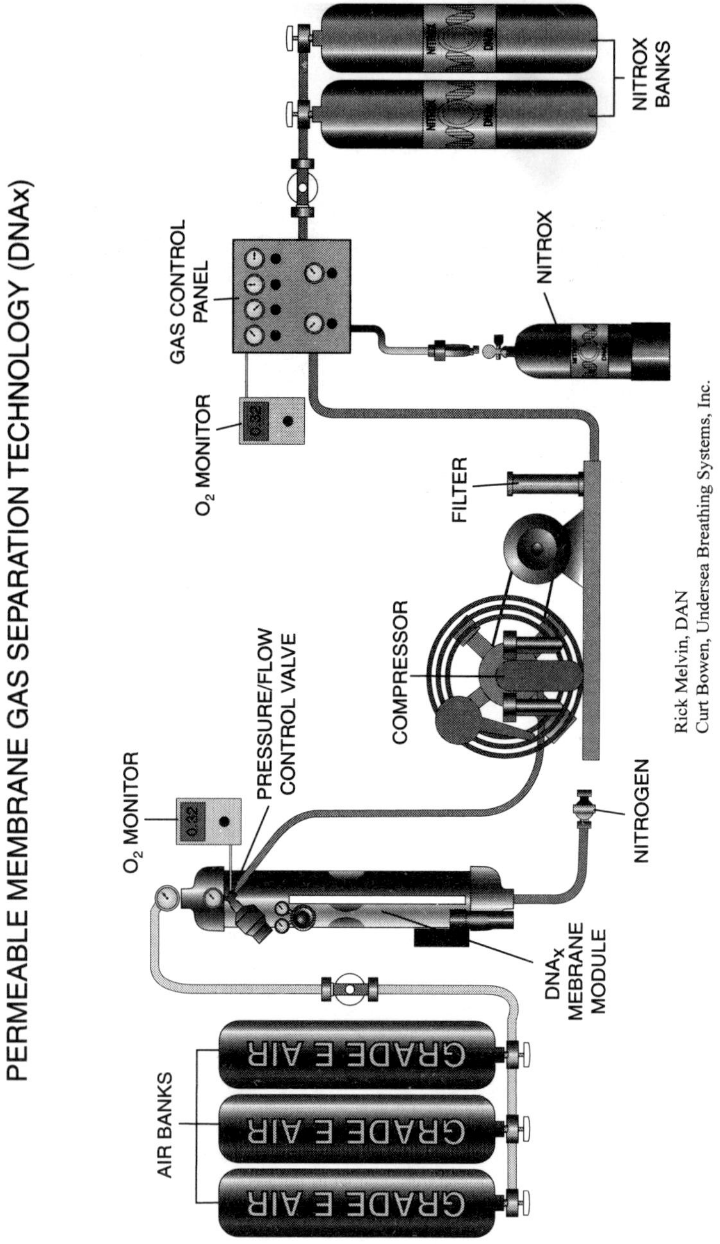

Figure 6-4
Typical DeNitrogenated Air (DNAx®) System

Among the advantages of PSA technology is its diversity. A PSA system can produce low pressure, high-purity oxygen; high-pressure air; or high-pressure nitrox. PSA systems currently under development will also be able to provide high-pressure oxygen, which can be used to charge rebreathers or for partial pressure blending of nitrox. PSA is a mature technology, dating back several decades. In fact, PSA systems have been used to provide breathing oxygen for jet fighter aircraft for nearly two decades. Molecular sieves are highly reliable, and with proper filtration of the inlet air, can easily last 10 to 15 years.

State-of-the-art PSA nitrox systems are generally designed for high volume production to meet the needs of a dive center or live-aboard dive boat. However, smaller systems are currently under development. A typical turnkey PSA system for a dive center, which can produce compressed air, high-purity oxygen, or nitrox, can be purchased for roughly the same cost as a typical high-pressure compressor system.

6.5 DNAx® TECHNOLOGY

Another process for making nitrox is referred to as DNAx® (DeNitrogenated Air, a registered trademark of Undersea Breathing Systems, Inc.) technology (figure 6-4). As with PSA, DNAx® removes nitrogen from air to produce nitrox. Rather than using a molecular sieve, DNAx® uses permeable membrane gas separation technology to remove nitrogen from ambient air at the molecular level. Instead of making high purity oxygen, the desired nitrox blend is produced directly using this nitrogen removal process.

The membrane module used for DNAx® is comprised of thousands of tiny hollow membrane fibers through which filtered air is pumped at a pressure of roughly 180 to 270 psig. Oxygen permeates or flows through the membrane at a higher rate than nitrogen due to surface chemistry phenomenon and the fact that the oxygen molecule is smaller than the nitrogen molecule. A valve on the product side of the membrane controls the flow of gas across the membrane, and precisely determines the oxygen/nitrogen ratio of the gas exiting the membranes. The higher the flow rate, the higher the ratio of oxygen in the exiting gas stream. The exiting air is compressed to the required pressure using a high-pressure compressor. An oxygen analyzer monitors the product gas, which then enters a compressor designed to bring the nitrox blend to the necessary pressure to fill cylinders.

Among the advantages of the DNAx® system is the fact that it can be operated in a manner that prevents the oxygen concentration from exceeding 40 percent anywhere in the system. Thus, a properly operated DNAx® system need not be oxygen clean. The membrane technology is also a mature technology requiring little maintenance. As long as the air entering the system is properly filtered and simple routine maintenance is accomplished, the membrane module can last up to 20 years or more.

Another advantage of the DNAx® technology is that it is compact, lightweight, and easily adapted to a portable nitrox generating system. A source of grade E air (scuba cylinders, a low-pressure compressor, etc.) may be required to provide the inlet air. Portable DNAx® systems are available in both gas and electric powered versions to produce nitrox at remote locations or aboard dive boats, and cost little more than a personal breathing air compressor.

CHAPTER 7

Safe Diving Considerations

If used properly and conservatively, recreational nitrox diving is no more dangerous than recreational diving with air. In some cases, nitrox can provide divers with an additional safety factor. However, additional precautions must be taken, and the same safe diving practices that apply to recreational air diving apply in spades to nitrox diving. Regardless of the nitrox blend used for diving, abide by the following safe diving considerations:

ALWAYS VERIFY THE OXYGEN CONTENT OF YOUR CYLINDER(S) BEFORE DIVING WITH NITROX. Verification should be done with the filling manifold removed from the cylinder, and cylinders should be reverified immediately prior to use. Remember that diving with the wrong mixture can result in serious complications including decompression illness and oxygen toxicity.

NEVER ATTEMPT TO BLEND YOUR OWN NITROX MIXTURES. Handling oxygen requires specialized skills and training to be accomplished safely. Leave it to the professionals — your life may depend on it.

NEVER FILL A NITROX CYLINDER WITH STANDARD BREATHING GRADE COMPRESSED AIR. Doing so will contaminate the cylinder, creating a serious hazard if the cylinder is later filled with nitrox. Likewise, never use a regular scuba cylinder for nitrox. Cylinders used for nitrox should be oxygen cleaned and properly labeled.

NEVER EXCEED THE MAXIMUM OPERATING DEPTH (MOD) OF A NITROX MIXTURE. Oxygen toxicity can be a serious threat, and can strike without warning. Follow the guidelines established by your certification agency, and always dive conservatively.

NEVER DIVE TO THE LIMITS. There is no black and white when it comes to no-decompression and oxtox limits. Considering all the potential variables for any diver on any day, diving to the no-decompression limit, or at the MOD for a nitrox mixture, is flirting with disaster. Leave yourself an extra margin for safety.

As a recreational nitrox diver, **NEVER ATTEMPT DECOMPRESSION DIVING,** even if it is within the capability of your dive computer.

KNOW YOUR COMPUTER. Nitrox computers require additional inputs not required by air-only dive computers. Errors in programming can result in serious consequences, including decompression illness and death.

NEVER DIVE ALONE. Diving alone poses a serious risk for recreational divers. Always dive with a properly trained, certified, and responsible buddy.

STAY CURRENT WITH YOUR DIVING. If you haven't been diving for six months or more, get refresher training through a professional scuba instructor before attempting an open water dive. If your nitrox diving knowledge is rusty, get a refresher from a certified nitrox instructor.

KNOW YOUR PERSONAL LIMITS AND STICK TO THEM. Divers must constantly assess their skills and abilities, and measure these against the multitude of variables anticipated for the particular diving environment. If a dive is beyond your skill, knowledge, or comfort level, or beyond those of your buddy, consider a new dive plan or location.

AVOID MEDICATIONS WHEN DIVING. The effects of increased pressure can alter the physiological response to certain medications. While much of the information on this subject is anecdotal, there is some evidence that certain medications including antihistamines can cause symptoms incompatible with safe diving, particularly when nitrox is used as the breathing gas. Before diving with any medication, consult your diving physician or contact the experts at the Divers Alert Network (DAN, 1-919-684-2928).

While every attempt has been made to provide accurate, up-to-date and easily understood material, the information contained in this manual is no substitute for training by a professional nitrox instructor. Before attempting to dive with nitrox, complete a nitrox diving certification course offered through a recognized certification agency.

Notes

Glossary

ABT
> Actual Bottom Time

ANDI
> American Nitrox Divers, Inc.

ATA
> Atmospheres absolute. A measurement of pressure equal to the standard atmospheric pressure, 14.7 psi, or 1 Bar.

Bar
> A metric unit of pressure measurement equal to standard atmospheric pressure.

Best Mix
> A term used to describe the nitrox blend having the highest possible oxygen content consistent with prescribed oxygen exposure limits at the maximum depth of the planned dive.

Blend
> A generic term used in reference to nitrox. The term blend is often used in conjunction with the percentage of oxygen in the breathing gas, e.g., a 34% blend refers to 34% oxygen or EAN 34.

Concentration
> The fraction or percentage of a gas in a breathing mixture.

Contents Tag
: A tag attached to a nitrox cylinder that lists the percentages of gasses in the blend.

DCIEM
: Defense and Civil Institute for Environmental Medicine

DNAx®
: Denitrogenated Air, a membrane gas separation technology commonly used to prepare nitrox.

EAD
: Equivalent Air Depth, the depth at which compressed air exerts the same partial of nitrogen as the nitrox blend under discussion, or the depth at which a diver breathing compressed air would experience the same nitrogen partial pressure as a diver breathing the reference nitrox blend at the actual depth.

EAN
: Enriched Air Nitrox, another pseudonym for nitrox.

END
: Equivalent Nitrogen Depth, same as EAD (Equivalent Air Depth).

FO_2
: An abbreviation for the fraction of oxygen present in a breathing gas mixture.

fsw
>Feet of sea water, used as a measure of depth in water.

IANTD
>International Association of Nitrox and Technical Divers

MEL
>Maximum Exposure Limit; generally refers to NOAA Single Dive Oxygen Exposure Limit.

Membrane System
>Refers to membrane gas separation technology used for preparing nitrox.

Mixture, Mix
>This term refers to the percentage or fraction of oxygen in a nitrox blend.

MOD
>Maximum Operating Depth; the maximum depth at which the specific nitrox blend can be used without exceeding a predetermined partial pressure of oxygen.

NAUI
>National Association of Underwater Instructors

NASDS
>National Association of Scuba Diving Schools

NDL
> No Decompression Limit, also no-stop limit. The maximum bottom allowed before a decompression stop is required.

NN32
> NOAA nitrox 32, a nitrox blend with 32% oxygen.

NN36
> NOAA nitrox 36, a nitrox blend with 36% oxygen.

NOAA
> National Oceanic and Atmospheric Administration

OCA
> Oxygen Compatible Air

OTU
> Oxygen Tolerance Unit, a measure of exposure to oxygen

Oxygen Clock
> A means of tracking or computing one's exposure to oxygen.

Oxtox
> Oxygen toxicity

Oxygen Analyzer
> A device, usually portable and hand-held, designed to measure the oxygen content of a breathing gas mixture.

Oxygen Cleaning

A process used to remove trace hydrocarbons, particulates, and other combustible materials that create a potential fire or explosion hazard. All equipment to be exposed to oxygen mixtures containing more than 40% oxygen must be oxygen cleaned.

Oxygen Compatible Air

Air from which trace contaminants have been removed making the air safe to mix with pure oxygen. Compressed Gas Association (CGA) Modified Grade E air is the standard for OCA.

Oxygen Toxicity

Adverse physiological responses to exceeding safe oxygen exposure limits. Oxygen toxicity can affect the central nervous system (CNS oxygen toxicity) and the lungs (pulmonary oxygen toxicity). Symptoms of oxygen toxicity include convulsions, visual disturbances, ringing of the ears, nausea, muscular tingling and twitching, irritability, dizziness, euphoria, coughing, and chest pain.

PADI

Professional Association of Diving Instructors

Partial Pressure
> The fraction of total pressure exerted by a specific gas in a mixture. The partial pressure of a gas is equal to the fraction of the gas in the mixture multiplied by the total pressure exerted by the mixture.

PO_2
> An abbreviation for the partial pressure of oxygen.

Partial Pressure Blending
> A technique for preparing nitrox in which pure oxygen and air are sequentially added to a nitrox cylinder. Partial pressure blending requires that the nitrox cylinder be oxygen cleaned.

PSA
> Pressure Swing Adsorption. A gas separation technology using molecular sieves commonly employed in the preparation of oxygen and nitrox.

Safe Air
> A pseudonym for nitrox. SafeAir is a copyrighted term used by American Nitrox Divers, Inc. (ANDI).

SSI
> Scuba Schools International

YMCA
> Young Men's Christian Association

References and Resources

The Annual Review of Recreational Scuba Diving Injuries Based on 1995 Data, Divers Alert Network, Durham, NC, 1997 Edition.

Bennett, Peter B., Ph. D., "Nitrox? Dr. Bennett Advises: Watch Your Safety Envelope," *Alert Diver,* March/April, 1998, Divers Alert Network, Durham, NC.

Brylske, Alex, Beating the Bends, Best Publishing, Flagstaff, AZ, 1999.

The DAN Annual Review of Recreational Scuba Diving Injuries Based on 1996 Data, Divers Alert Network, Durham, NC, 1998 Edition.

Donald, Kenneth, Oxygen and the Diver, Best Publishing, Flagstaff, AZ, 1992.

Dueker, Christopher W., Medical Aspects of Sport Diving, A. S. Barnes and Co., Inc., Cranbury, NJ, 1970.

McBride, William E., High Pressure Breathing Air Handbook, Best Publishing, Flagstaff, AZ, 1996.

<u>NOAA Diving Manual,</u> Fourth Edition, Best Publishing, Flagstaff, AZ, 2000.

<u>PADI Enriched Air Operations and Resource Guide,</u> International PADI.

Rossier, Robert N., <u>Dive Like a Pro: 101 Ways to Improve Your Scuba Skills and Safety,</u> Best Publishing, Flagstaff, AZ, 1999.

Rutkowski, Dick, <u>Enriched Air Nitrox Student Manual and Workbook,</u> International Association of Nitrox and Technical Divers, Miami Shores, FL, 4th Edition, 1995.

Thalmann, E. D., M.D., "If You Dive Nitrox, You Should Know About Oxtox," *Alert Diver,* May/June, 1997, Divers Alert Network, Durham, NC.

<u>U.S. Navy Diving Manual,</u> Best Publishing, Flagstaff, AZ.

Notes

Notes